Other Books by Norm Wright

Afraid No More
After You Say I Do
Always Daddy's Girl
Before You Remarry
Before You Say I Do
Chosen for Blessing
Communication: Key to Your Marriage
Communication: Key to Your Marriage Curriculum
Counseling and Testing Practical Applications
Crisis Counseling
Family Is Still a Great Idea
A Guidebook for Dating, Waiting, Choosing a Mate
Holding on to Romance
Help, I'm a Camp Counselor
How to Speak Your Spouse's Language
Kids Have Feelings Too (with Gary Oliver)
Making Peace with Your Past
Marital Counseling
More Communication Keys for Your Marriage
More Communication Keys for Your Marriage Curriculum
The Pillars of Marriage
Power of a Parent's Words
The Premarital Counseling Handbook
Pressure Points
Questions Women Ask in Private
Quiet Times for Couples
Recovering from the Losses of Life
Recovering from the Losses of Life Curriculum
Seasons of a Marriage
Self-Talk, Imagery, Prayer
So You're Getting Married
Training Christians to Counsel
When Anger Hits Home (with Gary Oliver)

NORM AND JOYCE WRIGHT

I'll Love You Forever

PUBLISHING

Colorado Springs, Colorado

I'LL LOVE YOU FOREVER

Library of Congress Cataloging-in-Publication Data
Wright, Norm, 1937—
    I'll love you forever / Norm and Joyce Wright.
        p.   cm.
    ISBN 1-56170-138-5
    1. Parent and child.   2. Parenting—Psychological aspects.
I. Wright, Joyce, 1937—   II. Title.
HQ755.85.W77   1993
306.874—dc20   93-10562
                                                                CIP

Published by Focus on the Family Publishing, Colorado Springs, Colorado 80995.
Distributed in the U.S.A. and Canada by Word Books, Dallas, Texas.

Certain details of case studies mentioned in this book have been changed to protect the privacy of the people involved.

Unless otherwise noted, Scripture quotations are from the HOLY BIBLE, NEW INTERNATIONAL VERSION®. Copyright © 1973, 1978, 1984 by the International Bible Society. Used by permission of Zondervan Publishing House. All rights reserved. Quotations identified NKJV are from the *New King James Version,* copyright © 1979, 1980, 1982 by Thomas Nelson, Inc., Publishers. Quotations identified NASB are from the New American Standard Bible, © 1960, 1962, 1963, 1968, 1971, 1972, 1973, 1975, 1977 by The Lockman Foundation. Quotations identified AMPLIFIED are from *The Amplified Bible,* © 1958, 1965 by the Lockman Foundation and Zondervan Publishing House.

Editor: Larry K. Weeden
Cover Design: Dale Fiorillo

Printed in the United States of America

93 94 95 96 97/10 9 8 7 6 5 4 3 2 1

To all those who stood with us in prayer and support during the growing years.

To those parents who are struggling with the unexpected challenges in their children's lives.

To Salem Christian Home and its staff for their faithful contribution to the care and growth of our son, Matthew.

Contents

One

Matthew's Story

THIS book is largely about someone God chose to use in a very different way. And this person never knew how or how much his life affected
others.

His impact came not so much from what he said, for that was very
limited. It wasn't so much what he did, either, for that, too, was very limited. In fact, that's the word that best describes him—*limited*—but perhaps only in the ways we think are the most significant. His calling was to
teach and refine those around him, and that he did, even though he
wasn't aware of it because his limitations got in the way.

This book, especially from an emotional standpoint, is about our son,
Matthew.

His limitations were actually what made him so effective. Had he
been what the world calls normal, our lives as parents would have been
less painful but so much more ordinary. God used him to make the truth
of Scripture more alive, more real, more relevant. He used him to teach
us to reevaluate our values, modify our expectations, appreciate aspects
of life taken for granted, become more fully human, and learn to grow
more dependent upon God. Perhaps what we have learned with
Matthew (and his sister, Sheryl) will be of help to you.

Have you ever wondered, when you're going through some experience, why it's happening and what you will learn from it? And then years
later you discovered the reason? Well, we certainly did.

After my (Norm's) graduation from Westmont College in 1959, we married, and I entered Fuller Seminary for two years. Prior to graduation from there, I had to write a master's thesis. I knew nothing about writing a thesis and didn't have the foggiest idea of what to write about. One of the unwritten rules at Fuller says, however, "Thou shalt never enter the professor's office and announce that you don't know what to write your thesis on, because said professor will assign you a topic no one has ever written on before."

Well, you've guessed it! I violated that rule, and I remember Dr. Price's telling me, "Norm, don't worry about it. I would like you to write a thesis on the Christian education of the mentally retarded child." Of course, I knew nothing about the subject.

I soon learned. I visited schools, churches, and homes, and I read and read. I wrote the thesis, Joyce typed it, and I turned it in. The professor gave it back to me for more work, I rewrote it, and Joyce retyped it. It was finally accepted, and I graduated.

After graduation, I joined a church staff and immediately entered another graduate program to earn a master's degree in clinical psychology. Four years later, in order to graduate, I needed to spend several hundred hours doing a school psychologist internship. When I walked into the school district office, I was assigned the task of testing and placing retarded students in their classes. Then the church learned about my experience in the school district and decided to develop a ministry to retarded children and their parents. I was given the job of selecting and training the teachers and developing the curriculum.

One day Joyce and I had one of the shortest conversations of our married life. It lasted less than 30 seconds, and we really don't remember who made the statement, but one of us said, "Isn't it interesting that we've had all this exposure to mentally retarded children and have learned so much about them? Could it be that God is preparing us for something that's going to occur later?"

That's all we said. Within a year our second child was born, a healthy, chubby boy we named Matthew.

Throughout this book, unless otherwise noted, the first-person singular references ("I did this," "I heard that") will be to Norm. But the remainder of this chapter will be Joyce's account of what happened with Matthew.

Something Is Very Wrong Here

As the weeks passed, Matthew seemed so easygoing and healthy. But at about five months, I noticed his lack of responsiveness. He seemed excessively sleepy, and his muscle tone was poor. His eyes didn't follow or track with us, and when I looked for his first smile, it wasn't there. I asked Norm if he noticed these things. He said he hadn't, but then he began to watch and confirmed what I was seeing. We both felt Matthew was okay, however. *He's just a little slower to begin with,* we thought. *He'll catch up in time.* At least that's what we told ourselves.

Yet as I continued to observe Matthew, my nagging doubts built up,

I knew instinctively that God was the only One who could give me the reassurance, comfort, and strength I needed.

and my fears soon overwhelmed me. I realized something was wrong, but I didn't know what.

I fell to my knees and told the Lord my fears. I asked Him, "Is something seriously wrong with my baby?"

I knew instinctively that God was the only One who could give me the reassurance, comfort, and strength I needed. He could understand my fear. No one else could reassure me (and I longed for reassurance) because the problem was undefined.

Although the Lord gave me His peace as I prayed, I knew in my heart that the problem with Matthew *was very real.* My mind in turmoil, I told God I could not raise this child without His strength and guidance each hour of every day. And thus I began to walk a special path of 22 years as a mom, learning to trust the Lord as never before. A passage that grew really special to me was Isaiah 43:2-5:

When you pass through the waters, I will be with you; and through the rivers, they shall not overflow you. When you walk through the fire, you shall not be burned, nor shall the flame scorch you. For I am the LORD your God, the Holy One of Israel, your Savior. . . . Since you were precious in My sight, you have been honored, and I have loved you. . . . Fear not, for I am with you. (NKJV)

I experienced many emotional ups and downs, but in my soul, I knew I could rely on God. Even though I was living in an intense time of uncertainty, He knew what was occurring. I had to trust in that fact; it was my lifeline.

Not long after that, Norm and I were away at a conference. We had left Matthew with my mother. While we were gone, he had some kind of seizure and stiffened in her arms. More and more, we were getting confirmation that we had a major problem.

Matthew was nine months old when I saw his first grand mal seizure. His entire body stiffened, his arms and legs jerked uncontrollably, and his eyes rolled back in his head. Seeing a convulsion in your child for the first time is terrifying! We were outside with a neighbor, and I had no clue what to do. The only thing I could think to do was to pray with my eyes open, in Jesus' name, while cradling Matthew in my arms. I felt *utterly helpless*. I will never forget that day, though I've often wished I could. Finally, the seizuring stopped, and I thanked God it was over.

Norm was away at Green Oaks Boys Camp training counselors. When he rushed home in response to my emergency call, I blurted out, "Why weren't you with me? Why weren't you here when we needed you?" He looked so puzzled and vulnerable. I could see my question was unreasonable, because the seizure lasted only a few minutes. From then on, I realized that when a seizure did come, I was not alone. It was the Lord, Matthew, and me.

Gradually, my confidence and faith were built up as we three weathered each episode. In the past, I had been a very dependent wife, so I needed to learn to be more independent when Norm was busy or away in his ministry. The Lord was obviously refining me to be the wife and mother He wanted me to be.

Matthew had more seizures, so we placed him under the care of neurologists at the UCLA Medical Center. After extensive testing, the doctor told us, "For some reason, something happened with the development of Matthew's brain, and that accounts for the severity of the retardation. And then at birth, further brain damage occurred somehow, which accounts for the seizure condition. Matthew may develop into a two-year-old mentally someday, and then again, he may not."

There it was. The diagnosis was definite, a confirmation of our worst fears. We were sent home with the news. Even though we weren't surprised, we were thunderstruck. Our precious boy was so sweet, so wonderful in so many ways, and yet our hopes and dreams for him now lay in ruins. A few words from a doctor had torn them apart, and nothing would ever put them back together.

In the months and years ahead, we had to make many more adjustments than we could ever have imagined. For example, we had to be more cautious with Matthew than we had been with his sister. We were constantly on the lookout for seizures. We were less likely to have baby-sitting available to us, and we had to be highly selective in choosing sitters.

Because of his disability, when Matthew reached preschool age, he couldn't attend regular classes. And even then, he was ill so much of the time and often so drowsy that he didn't benefit much from his special classes. We also had to explain to others why he didn't respond like other children. (When Matthew was an infant and preschooler, his disabilities were not immediately evident. But if you were around him for a while, his lack of alertness became apparent.) And over the years, we had to go through the process of obtaining state funding for his training—and then speak up for him every time the state decided to cut back on funds for the developmentally disabled.

Our church had no facilities for a child like Matthew, either. He also had to be carried for years. Consequently, whenever we took him anywhere, we had to carry lots of extra equipment.

As the years went by, the daily grind really got to me. For all the reasons mentioned above, I was exhausted, discouraged, and isolated at home much of the time. I had little energy left to go out socially or even relax. I wondered if my endless list of chores was really important. My focus was on the daily care of Matthew, Sheryl, and Norm—and not much else.

Sometimes when I was discouraged, the Lord ministered to me as I listened to old hymns, their familiar words building up my faith. That was when I could let the tears flow. I needed it so much because I tried to keep my composure for the sake of the rest of the family. When I found I could sing along and mean it, my day would lighten a great deal. It helped to look back and remember God's faithfulness and the significant things He had brought us through. Matthew had many illnesses and frequent high temperatures and seizures, but then there would be a wonderful answer to prayer.

We developed a new sense of appreciation for each small sign of progress. It took Matthew more than two years before he first reached out to grasp an object. Instead of taking that for granted as we had with Sheryl, we praised God for it. It was a step in the right direction.

We prayed for more than three years for Matthew to walk. I had seen some tottering steps at the developmental school where they were trying to teach him. One evening, all of us were sitting in the living room, and Matthew stood up, took four steps, and plopped down. Norm and I made some profound remark like "Isn't that great?" But our ten-year-old daughter said, "Why don't we stop right now and thank God for answering this prayer?" So we did.

In many ways, we continued with life. Our vacation time was important, so in the summer we would load our car with Portacrib, stroller, playpen, and everything else and head for Montana to visit Norm's brother's family, or go to Grand Teton National Park in Wyoming to fish. And when I say we stayed in a small, rustic cabin in Wyoming, I mean small and rustic! The first was no larger than 10 by 12 feet, and that was the first year it had electricity. The bathrooms were in a central location, and we hauled in water from the stream nearby. We always had to check first to make sure moose weren't standing in the water. That was when we discovered Matthew was allergic to mosquito bites.

The vacations were a mixture of enjoyment, confinement, and hard work, but they were significant for all of us. Sheryl said those were her most enjoyable times with Matthew. A few years later, Norm realized those trips weren't always a vacation for me, and we made some changes.

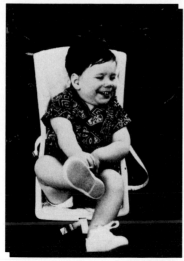

Matthew as a happy six-month-old.

Sheryl and Matthew when she was nine and he was three.

Eight-year-old Matthew with Prince, our shelty.

Enjoying Christmas at home when Matthew was 14.

Matthew's graduation at age 21.

We were very selective about baby-sitters for Matthew, but the Lord pro-vided a retired Christian nurse who could stay with Matthew for extended periods while we went north. What a difference it made to have a real break from the daily responsibility!

At times I experienced an overwhelming exhaustion. Some nights Matthew sat up and jabbered and squealed, and I didn't get much sleep. Over the years, we worked with various medications to try to control his seizures, and it was a battle to maintain a balance and not have him under or overmedicated. Often we had to deal with various side effects as

The Lord was using our circumstances to glorify His name. That's what it was all about.

well. The doctors told me I probably would know better than anyone the level of medication that would be best for Matthew, so it was up to me to experiment and determine that level. This sometimes seemed to be an overwhelming responsibility.

One Sunday, I dropped into an adult Sunday school class and heard Norm teaching. He was telling about Matthew's life and how the Lord was refining us by the presence of this precious child in our home. For me, it was like opening a door to a whole new world of spiritual under-standing. The Lord was using our circumstances to glorify His name. That's what it was all about. It meant so much to me to know that God was working out His purpose in our lives.

We've also been amazed, over the years, by the way Matthew's story has touched people at such a tender, deep level, even though they never met him. Being the parents of a disabled child has forced us to learn to walk each day by faith, and our going through that process has been a clear testimony of God's grace.

Matthew had a special innocence about him, with an easygoing man-ner. He was happy and content wherever he was. After our very active Sheryl, I delighted in holding and comforting this sweet child who needed me so much. It was a joy to do some of the most basic things for him. Many people prayed faithfully for him, and I believe God walked with him—he had such a sweet spirit.

God provided three main people to walk beside me and give me input and strength. The primary person was Norm. He was committed to loving and raising our disabled child. I was assured early on that I could count on him. He was a zealous provider, juggling many jobs, sometimes working too much, and yet he was there to encourage me when I had doubts or needed a more objective view. The Lord had entrusted me with an awesome responsibility as Matthew's mother, and Norm was supportive and let me lead in his care. Norm was very much the head of our home in all areas, especially with our bubbly Sheryl.

Norm is also fun-loving, and he filled our house with positive attitudes. With our first child, I tended to be a rather serious mom, and Norm's sense of humor boosted my outlook. With two children, I learned to see the humor in some of our daily experiences with a disabled child. We could be a silly group on occasion, which helped us to be less stressed out.

One of our funny episodes was quite frustrating at the time! Matthew and I were home sick from church on a Sunday, and Norm and Sheryl were still away. I did what I tend to do frequently: I locked myself out of the house. (I have keys everywhere now.) Still in my robe, I was on my way to the garage with another load of diapers for the washer. I tried the door. It wouldn't open. I looked in the door window, and my key wasn't where it should be. I saw the dog; he was licking Matthew's face. And Matthew was serenely chewing on a bar of soap in his zip-up sleeper!

Oh, no! I thought. *Norm and Sheryl won't be home for hours.* So I got the screwdriver, took off the molding around the doggie door, and squeezed through. If I had to try that now, there is no way I could fit!

Another time, we had guests for dinner, and I had fixed a dessert with blueberries and cream on top of the glass dessert dish. Matthew ambled by Norm's uncle, and since no one was watching, he reached out and swept the top of that dessert off the dish and into his mouth. Many times, he outsmarted the dog and cat and ate their food as well!

On another occasion, the cat was asleep in a recliner. Matthew walked up and grabbed its tail with a viselike grip. The cat immediately came alive, leapt from the chair, and ran full speed across the room.

Matthew forgot to let go, and the cat literally dragged him across the room. His laughter rang through the house with his free ride.

The second person who was so important to me was my mother. She has been a wonderful example of trusting God each day, standing on Scripture during her son's bout with cancer and early death. I was a young wife, spiritually immature, and had no experience with deep trouble. So watching my mother made a great impression on me. I saw God transform my brother's rebellious life, and I learned to look past the circumstances of illness and death to spiritual victory. I saw my mother hang in there through very trying times. I knew her way was the only way I could get through my own tremendous challenge.

The third person God brought into my life was my best friend, Fran. Norm has a lot of friends, but I've had a tendency to be shy and a bit of a loner. Being married to an outgoing husband and minister and being home most of the time with a disabled child didn't help me to grow in that area.

Fran had been my best friend since college. In Matthew's early years, she would call me as the Lord put me on her heart. Even though she had no disabled children, she was incredibly sensitive to what I was going through, and she would let me bare my soul. I can share anything with her, and she will listen sensitively and say, "Now we need to pray." Then we will pray on the phone, back and forth, until our prayer list is finished.

By the time Matthew was eight, my life seemed to be in constant crisis. He had frequent infections and high fevers that kept him out of his specialized school for weeks, and Norm worked long hours and continued to travel in his ministry. All that kept me off balance. Either Matthew was sick and needed a tepid bath in the middle of the night, or Norm was leaving for a seminar. In my most honest moments of self-talk, I wondered how much longer I could keep going. I was growing numb to life around me, with very little interest or enthusiasm. Both Norm and Sheryl noticed the frustration in my voice and became concerned.

A Hard Decision

One day I met a friend at the local drugstore. I was there to get antibiotics for Matthew's latest infection. She had placed her son in a home for the disabled. I could see what a positive step it was for her. I was genuinely happy for her, but I was sure I would never do that with Matthew. I thought her circumstances were a lot different. Her son was hyper, so her house was frantic all the time. My little guy was sweet and easygoing, and I just would never do it. But the next time I ran into her, I was again getting antibiotics, and I was exhausted. I had been up long hours with Matthew, fighting high temperatures. I wondered if there was a solution for us. I looked at her, and she seemed so rested, peaceful, and happy. What was God's will for Matthew?

Norm and I began to ask, "What's best for him? What's best for us? Could someone else help him develop more than we can? Could someone else help him to lie down and sleep more at night, eat better, and learn some everyday skills? Could that someone give him better constant care than we can?"

This process of questioning and searching occurred over a period of three years as we prayed, looked, and waited. We began to consider the possibility of a small, Christian residential facility for Matthew. We would not place him in a state institution. Eventually we discovered Salem Christian Home, which is run by the Christian Reformed denomination in Ontario, California. We took Matthew for an evaluation, and the staff said he would be a good fit in their multidisability ward. They would put him on the waiting list, and we could expect to wait from one to five years.

While we waited, I felt defeated in Matthew's care. He didn't eat well. I couldn't get him to lie down and sleep. He would sit up and giggle all night, leaving Norm and me exhausted the next day. We felt totally helpless to change the situation. I began to call the home, desperate for practical advice, and I soon realized the staff had knowledge that was workable. I saw they could give him better care than just one mom could manage.

A year later, we received a call saying the home was ready for Matthew. All of a sudden, the time had come. We talked about how the change would affect us. There were so many positives to look forward to, but we had concerns as well: "What if our identity was largely based on caring for a disabled, dependent child? If he is no longer a part of our daily lives, how will we feel about ourselves?" Many parents, especially mothers, struggle with these issues when their children leave home. We also wondered if Matthew would forget us. Because of his limited mental ability, that was a real possibility.

We began preparations for taking him, and then the first disappointment hit. He came down with pneumonia, and his leaving was delayed. Weeks later, he was well again, but the state funding had not yet come through, and the move was postponed again. Once the funding was approved and we had the go-ahead, Matthew became ill with mononucleosis.

Not only were we disappointed, but now we began to question whether we had misread God's leading. Were we right or not? Then, when Matthew was well, the home called and said we had to wait again since they were quarantined for two weeks. We really struggled with what was right to do. We felt as though we were on an emotional roller coaster.

Finally, everything was ready. We packed and took Matthew to the home, unpacked his things, and said good-bye. We wouldn't be able to see him for the adjustment period of six weeks. As we drove away, both Norm and I had such a sense of peace and calm that we began to feel guilty about it.

What was wrong with us? We had just relinquished the care of our son to others for the rest of our lives, and we didn't feel upset or a sense of loss! And then it hit us. God, in His wisdom, had allowed us to go through those delays for several months, and we had worked out our feelings and adjustment in advance. And with the delays, instead of Matthew's being placed during the winter, at the height of the cold and flu season, the placement occurred during the summer, when he and the other residents had a greater chance of being well. There was a purpose. We saw that God not only prepared us for Matthew's arrival, but also for the time when we would relinquish him to the care of others.

After Matthew's placement at Salem, I experienced an incredible lifting of my spirit, because I was released from the physical demands of his care. I slept like never before, felt well, and looked around at my world with wonder and awe. Norm, Sheryl, and Fran's family were all good to me. They sensed it could be a rough time. I now had the opportunity, however, for my personality to develop and blossom. For 11 years, it was as if I had taken a detour from life to carry a heavy but very special responsibility, and I needed to reorient myself to life.

Before long, we could see that Matthew was well, gaining weight, and in school more consistently. When he visited us at home, he seemed brighter and more alert. Life was obviously more meaningful for him.

He learned so much at Salem! He learned to walk up stairs, turn on a faucet, dog paddle in a pool, and feed himself. (Three bites out of five hitting the mouth aren't bad!) He didn't forget us, and he maintained his good-natured disposition. He seemed to enjoy music, and now and then he would sit at the piano and bang on the keys. Occasionally, he would throw his head back and laugh and clap his hands.

One of our most precious gifts from Matthew was his learning to hug.

As Matthew grew older, he rarely cried. But when he did, his sense of helplessness tore us apart.

We would bring Matthew home at least once a month. We looked forward to his visits and always hoped he would be both well and alert. On many occasions, Norm drove out by himself and brought Matthew home, which was a help. He would talk to Matthew on the way and try to keep him awake, since he tended to fall asleep when he rode. Sometimes I would meet them at the car, but other times Norm would open the door, and Matthew would walk through the house to the family room and curl up in the big chair. Then I would act surprised when I walked in, and I would rush over to hug him. Once in a while, he would seem to recognize me and giggle, but other times he made little response.

Matthew appeared to be comfortable and peaceful whether he was home with us or at Salem. Each time we took him back to Salem, he was content and satisfied. Fortunately, he never cried because he didn't want to be left there—that would have really hurt us.

One of our most precious gifts from Matthew was his learning to hug. For 15 years, we never received any response when we held him. We realize he was limited because his mental development never seemed to progress beyond an 18-month-old level. But something happened, and occasionally when we hugged him—perhaps two or three times a year—we would feel his arms around us, hugging us in return. And sometimes when we would look at him, open our arms, and say, "Matthew, hug," he would come to us with arms open in response. You can't imagine how we valued those responses! How unfortunate that most people tend to take loving touches for granted.

We had a joyful, thankful response to everything positive about Matthew's life and made sure we shared it with others so God would be glorified. Answers to prayer confirmed to us that the Lord was blessing the placement. At times when Matthew was ill or had problems, a rush of mothering feelings would surface, and some of the old feelings of concern and helplessness would return. Staying involved on the phone with the nursing staff helped me, and they gladly cooperated with my desire for that.

As a mother, I still had my responsibilities, and with good energy and great joy I picked out Matthew's new clothes, went to school and home meetings, and planned for his home visits. At times it was hard to step back into his world. His needs were so basic and his response so limited. We saw the enormity of his disabilities even more objectively.

My self-talk was really important after Matthew's placement, because there were rough times. I would tell myself, *I've done the best I can for these 11 years,* and I would gratefully acknowledge that the Lord's strength had sustained me. *And now the Lord has led us to place him at Salem, and it's time for others to meet his needs.* It helped to remind myself of that. At times I needed to remind myself, too, that the larger staff could do more than I ever could. I had to adjust to the fact that their care wasn't just like home and to look for the signs of improvement—to consider the overall picture. I'd often start the day by saying, "Thank You, Lord, for the fine care You've provided for Matthew this day."

Even though I felt a deep longing to be with Matthew, I felt a sense of relief that I no longer had to try to provide all his physical care. But there were times when I saw a disabled child with his mom in a store and experienced overwhelming feelings of loss and guilt. Then, realizing we couldn't go shopping together due to the magnitude of Matthew's disabilities, I would admit, *Yes, I wish we were together, but I'm thankful God has provided.* When I told Norm about this mixture of feelings, he was very supportive and assured me it was perfectly normal and okay.

We have learned so much over the years. Perhaps some of it can best be summed up in this statement written years ago by a brother in Christ:

> The retarded are the sign that all men have significance beyond what they can be, and do for us. To see the retarded honestly is to remind us that we cannot earn significance for our lives, it is a gift of God. Christ makes it possible for us to love our retarded brothers in a way radically different from the possessive love that thrives on the need to be needed. To love the weak in Christ is to dare to be free and to dare to be free from dependency on their needs. God wants us to see each other as significant only as we exist in Him. We are each God's gift to the other.[1]

Difficulties of Many Kinds

Now you know a lot more about Matthew and our experiences with him, and perhaps you can understand better why we care so much about hurting parents. But having a disabled child is only one form of loss or disappointment that comes because our kids can't or choose not to live up to our expectations. And in this book, we want to explore the impact of all those losses on ourselves as individual parents, on our marriages, and on other children in the family. In the next chapter, for example, we'll consider the child who wanders away from parental values.

Our prayer—our reason for reliving our pain to write this book—is that you will see your own situation in these pages, draw comfort from the knowledge that we share your hurt, and find battle-tested wisdom to help you through your trials. In the end, you can even come out stronger for the experience. Ultimately, that means learing to draw on the strength and love of the Lord, and most of all we want to see you grow closer to Him.

~Two~
The Wandering Child

ANOTHER kind of loss and hurt can also disrupt your life as a parent. You know it happens to other families, but you don't expect it to invade your household. At least, you hope it doesn't. It's a shock when that child for whom you've had such high hopes turns her back on your values, your teaching, and the Lord.

It often begins with a phone call. You pick up the phone, and the caller identifies himself and proceeds to tell you something about your son or daughter that you simply cannot believe. The person could be a police officer, teacher, pastor, friend, or newspaper reporter. Or your son or daughter may call you directly or tell you the situation in person. All too often, the words cause shock, disbelief, and dismay. Some of the last words a parent ever wants to hear may be heard:

"Mom, I'm gay."

"Mom, I'm pregnant."

"Dad, I'm living with my girlfriend."

"Dad, I was busted for selling coke."

"I'm moving out."

"I'm dropping out of school. It's a waste, and I won't graduate anyway."

"I'm in the hospital. I tried to take my life."

"I'm in the hospital. I had an abortion, and there's a problem."

"I have AIDS."

Such words shake the very foundations of a home and family. Everything you've worked for, prayed for, and sacrificed for has just crumbled.

You're a hurting parent. Buddy Scott describes well why you hurt:

You hurt . . .

- because the children you love have turned toward self-destruction.
- because your children stand in grotesque defiance against you.
- because your megacontribution to the lives of your kids is not being appreciated by them.

You hurt . . .

- because you feel like failures as parents.
- because you are haunted by your thoughts, *If only we had done this or not done that.*
- because other parents—some with younger children or some fortunate enough not to have had severe problems with their teenagers—look at you like you are failures.
- because you are frustrated from going behind your kids cleaning up their messes.
- because you have to mix with people at work, at community functions, or at church who know about your children's problems.
- because you wonder if you ought to give up your positions at church or in the community.

You hurt . . .

- because you don't know for sure how to help your children.
- because you don't know what to do or how to think.[1]

Our many joyful experiences with our children produce a reservoir of fond memories. I often reflect on them, as you probably do, too. Do you remember those first days of school when your child came racing home to share his or her exciting discoveries? I do. I also remember watching our five-year-old daughter bait her own hook with a live anchovy on a deep-sea boat, toss the bait into the water, and reel in her fish all by herself. That trip led to many experiences of hiking and boating with her throughout Montana and Wyoming.

I think of her final piano recital when she was in high school. She talked me into playing a duet with her for her last number. It was supposed to be a serious recital, but we soon destroyed that image. As we played, the music slid off the piano into our laps, and we couldn't stop laughing until we concluded the piece. I'm glad that happened, because the event is much more vivid in my memory than it would have been otherwise.

I also remember listening to Sheryl describe how she invited Jesus Christ into her life and the joy I experienced over that. Perhaps you've had that experience with your child.

You feel shattered when the dreams you've had for your children are destroyed. You want the best for them. You want them to be well-adjusted and happy. You have hopes for their occupations, their spouses, their children, their accomplishments, and their Christian life.

But sometimes the dreams have an extra dimension to them. You invest so deeply in them because some are really your own unfulfilled dreams or unbending expectations. I've talked with numerous parents

> *I've talked with numerous parents who were living their lives through their children.*

who were living their lives through their children. What they couldn't experience or accomplish would be fulfilled vicariously through their children. There was no thought that it wouldn't happen; it was set in concrete, at least in the minds of the parents.

That's a dangerous approach, however. What happens when your kids' free will and personal desires kick in and override your wishes? This can happen in their desire not to pursue Little League, soccer, or piano lessons, as well as in major moral choices that counter all you've been trying to instill for years. When your dreams, plans, goals, and desires are rejected, you end up feeling wounded.

One writer had an insightful perspective on this issue. He said:

> Many parents see their children as extensions of themselves, or as their possessions, or as the fulfillment of their unfulfilled lives. These are all potentially destructive attitudes to have toward raising one's children. All of these "beliefs" make children into "little idols" in one form or another. We "idolize" them. We hallow them and their achievements. We have to, because we have invested so much of ourselves in them. Such idolatry, created by unresolved grief, not only blocks grieving, but blocks the opportunity to discover our children as adults.
>
> The central theological question is: "Whom do our children belong to?" For people of faith, the answer should be: God. Isn't that what we acknowledge in infant baptism or dedication? God gives them to us as gifts. They are on loan. Our job is to raise them, teach them, love them and then launch them into the world, thereby returning them to God. They are with us only for a short time.[2]

Without stretching the issue too much, you end up feeling abused and victimized. One parent said, "I feel like I'm going through a divorce, not by my spouse but by my 17-year-old. Our relationship has crumbled. He won't even talk to us anymore, let alone listen to any suggestions or even help. And I've pretty well planned on burying all my hopes for him going to that Christian college. He won't go to church anymore. He told me he doesn't even believe anymore. Maybe I ought to have a funeral service for the future! It sure looks dead to me!"

And your struggles and pain intensify each day. You may feel a bit intimidated because you're not sure what to do. That's the usual concern I hear when parents come to my office. You may also feel intimidated because you don't agree with your partner on what to do.

Buddy Scott talks about the struggle with a rebelling adolescent:

But perhaps the scariest intimidation is the risk involved in demanding appropriate behavior. You may be afraid that your action might cause your children to . . .

run away
drop out of school
fail to graduate from high school and college
lose their jobs
talk against you to significant others
report you to child welfare for child abuse
turn further away from you and toward the wrong crowd
get deeper into drugs
get someone pregnant or get pregnant
and so forth

Defiant and rebellious kids become aware of your dreadful anxieties and use them against you. *They will sometimes grab hold of your fears and use them as tools of manipulation to further intimidate you. They threaten to make your worst fears come true if you continue to interfere in their lives.* You may be left shivering in swamps of despair.

Abused parents can be benched by the anxieties that spew from in*timid*ation.

Abused parents are often benched by anxiety attacks. You sometimes sit with your head in your hands bewildered about what to do. You feel powerless, confused, and guilty.

It's as if you have become an *invalid* parent. Just think of what the word *invalid* means: "Having become incapable of caring for oneself, sick." Another meaning of *invalid* is "nonvalid, not worth anything."[3]

You do feel immobilized. We know. We felt that way during the first few months our daughter was away from the Lord (more about that shortly). You feel torn between wanting to do something that will work and not wanting to do anything that will make the situation worse. Sometimes the pain is so intense because you're left in the dark. You don't know what's going on with your child. Part of you wants all the details, and part of you is afraid of hearing the worst. In one way we were fortunate, because the lines of communication between Sheryl and us were never cut off. We usually knew what was going on, and sometimes that intensified our pain, because it heightened our feelings of helplessness.

"I'm Living with My Boyfriend"

One of my most difficult tasks as a father and husband was having to tell Joyce what was occurring with our daughter. Sheryl had made an appointment to see me at the end of my office hours one day, but I didn't know that until I went out to the desk and glanced at my appointment book. I was surprised to see Sheryl's name written in. I went back into my office, and she was sitting there quietly, waiting for me.

I was puzzled about why she was there, and for the first few minutes, nothing significant seemed to transpire. But then she said, " The reason I'm here, Daddy, is that I've never lied to you and Mother before, and I'm not going to now. I wanted to let you and Mother know that I'm living with my boyfriend."

We continued to talk calmly. I told her I appreciated her telling me directly so I wouldn't hear about it from someone else. But already a sense of weight and dread was creeping through my emotions.

We parted, and I went outside, got in my car, and just sat there for a moment. Numbness from the shock settled in as I drove home. I relived the conversation a dozen times or more. Perhaps part of the reason I went through it so many times had to do with hope. I was hoping I would discover it was all a bad dream, that it hadn't happened and wasn't true. And by rehashing it again and again, I was probably delaying what I knew was inevitable—having to tell Joyce.

I started to formulate and rehearse what I was going to say to her. I wanted to postpone and avoid it. I didn't want to inflict what I knew would be an incredible amount of pain on her. That evening and the next day, I started to tell her several times, but each time I pulled back and waited. Finally, I told her I needed to reveal something to her, and I did. I could see the impact it had on her, and I wished again that it wasn't true and that I didn't have to be the one to tell her.

Joyce's response, though, was different from what I had anticipated. The news confirmed where she felt Sheryl's path had been leading. Joyce was more hurt and sad rather than stunned, because she knew such a life-style wouldn't bring Sheryl happiness. Joyce also realized Sheryl had made a conscious decision to step out of God's will, so she began to firmly pray against that choice.

For the next four years, we felt as though we were in an emotional Death Valley. It was the most difficult time in our parenting role since we placed Matthew in his home two years before. We seemed to go from one crisis to another during that period. We experienced situations that we had heard of in the lives of other families but had never anticipated occurring in our own.

Who would have thought that one of Sheryl's fiancés would turn out to be a drug dealer and physical abuser? We didn't, nor did she. Who would have thought that we would receive a call from her to come and move her home because of a difficult situation with her female room-mate who was dealing drugs? That was one time when we felt more of a sense of control, because we were able to report the person to the authorities.

*F*or the next four years, we felt as though
we were in an emotional Death Valley.

Despite the pain, we spent many enjoyable hours with Sheryl that gave us hope for our relationship. But overall it was a time of sadness, because we saw no indication that she might reverse her course of action. We were often tempted to point out the pitfalls of what she was doing and correct her. Most of the time we kept quiet, however, because our mentioning the situation only aroused her defensiveness. And then we learned that she was already struggling under a load of guilt and certainly didn't need more.

Too often the parents carry the load of guilt and self-blame. Perhaps the more determined you are that your child will be a certain way, the more intense the pain. I've heard parents say, "What went wrong?" And in time I hear, "What did I do wrong? Where did I blow it?" Mothers especially feel this way and are quicker to admit it than fathers. Each parent has to confront and work through his or her feelings of guilt. The author of *Mother, I Have Something to Tell You* talked about this universal struggle:

> The mother's dilemma in a nutshell: "I did something or I didn't do something." What mother can ever be sure that what she is doing—or not doing—with her child is right, unmistakably, irrefutably right, at any given moment?
>
> This guilt has been unfairly augmented by so-called experts. Dr. Paula Caplan and Dr. Ian Hall-McCorquodale, of the Ontario Institute for Studies in Education, recently reviewed one hundred and twenty-five articles in journals of clinical psychology from 1970, 1976, and 1982. They found "mother-blaming" rampant, regardless of the sex of the author, the type of journal, and the year of publication. Seventy-two kinds of disorders were directly attributed to mothers. Mothers were related to a child's problems five times as often as fathers.
>
> The time has come to take mothers off the hook. Successful mothering depends on a mysterious anagram of personality and circumstance. What works with one child will not work with his sister. In the families described here, children who are now happy, independent, and productive grew up with brothers or sisters whose lives seem to their mothers to be, to use a word that keeps recurring in these interviews, "wasted." And, as different as the children have turned out, the mother is not aware of having treated them in the least differently when they were growing up. In fact, the child who comes to grieve the mother most may have been the one who showed the most promise. Because they are curious and courageous, the most promising children often behave the least traditionally. They have everything going for them—intelligence, talent, concern for others, an appetite for life. They are accustomed to success. Small wonder that these young people are so often the ones who find defying tradition easy and tempting.

When they succeed, their mother does not take the credit. When they fail, should she take the blame? Whatever other questions a mother may ask the experts as she begins to pay attention to her child as he really is, the one great spoken or unspoken question for every mother is, "Is it my fault?"

The answer she gets depends on which expert she asks.[4]

It's normal to look at yourself and begin to blame. Yet even though we are all imperfect as parents (and some perhaps more than others!), the rebellion of your children doesn't mean you're a failure as a parent. My worth and your worth are not based on the choices our children make.

Who can explain why four children in a family have healthy attitudes and are morally responsible—but one rebels? We're dealing with birth order, personality differences, neurological structure, an inordinate amount of peer pressure, a non-Christian moral system in our society, and their own free will. If you are raising your kids to be Christians and reflect that value system, you are raising them to be minority individuals in a hostile environment.

Recently, I talked with Sheryl about her wandering years. As we discussed why they happened, she made an interesting observation: "Part of it was peer pressure, but I've come to realize that when you have an artistic bent such as I do, but don't have the opportunity to express yourself in that way, you tend to move more toward drugs and alcohol. At that time I didn't feel I could go ahead and express myself with my art as I can now, and I think that had something to do with it." She also mentioned finding a shirt with a statement written on it that she connected with immediately. It read, "Art and music are the drugs of choice for thousands of kids. If we expect them to just say no to a chemical high, we must recognize the healing alternative, their own creativity. Demand and support the real anti-drug program—arts in education."

Now when Sheryl feels stress and tension, she can both pray about it and create a painting that fulfills her need.

What the Bible Really Says

Ezekiel 18 is helpful in assessing blame for the rebellious behavior of grown children. God's way of looking at that situation is clear:

> The word of the LORD came to me: "What do you people mean by quoting this proverb about the land of Israel: 'The fathers eat sour grapes, and the children's teeth are set on edge'? As surely as I live, declares the Sovereign LORD, you will no longer quote this proverb in Israel. For every living soul belongs to me, the father as well as the son—both alike belong to me. The soul who sins is the one who will die." (Ezek. 18:1-4)

Then in verse 20 He concludes, "The son will not share the guilt of the father, nor will the father share the guilt of the son. The righteousness of the righteous man will be credited to him, and the wickedness of the wicked will be charged against him."

Your family isn't the only one to be traumatized. So was God's, and right from the beginning. He loved Adam and Eve, but He lost them. He spent time with them, but they succumbed to temptation. He confronted them, and they blamed others. God was the first parent to be blamed, too. Adam said, "The woman You gave to me did it." God under-

*The proverbs were never intended to be absolute **promises** from God. Instead, they're **probabilities** of things that are likely to occur.*

stands what you're experiencing. He gave Adam and Eve a perfect environment, perfect teaching, and perfect love, and there was still no guarantee they would choose to follow His guidelines.

If there's one passage I've heard used and misused and misinterpreted time and again, it's Proverbs 22:6: "Train a child in the way he should go, and when he is old he will not turn from it." God never intended that verse to be a guarantee that children raised faithfully would be godly. In fact, the writers of Proverbs were fully aware that godly parents might have ungodly children. Otherwise, they would not have said, "Whoever loves wisdom makes his father rejoice, but a companion of harlots wastes his wealth" (Prov. 29:3, NKJV). This proverb and others like it (see, e.g., 10:5) face reality: Children can reject their parents' moral and spiritual training.

The writers also admitted that children may curse their parents: "There is a generation that curses its father, and does not bless its mother. There is a generation that is pure in its own eyes, yet is not washed from its filthiness" (Prov. 30:11-12, NKJV).

Children, according to the book of Proverbs, may also despise their parents (see 15:20) and mock them (see 30:17). Children raised in a godly home may waste their parents' money (see 28:24) and even refuse to help a widowed mother in need of food and housing (see 19:26).

The writers of Proverbs reflected life as they experienced it (after humanity's fall into sin) and not as a fantasy existence. So what do we make of Proverbs 22:6?

The proverbs were never intended to be absolute promises from God. Instead, they're probabilities of things that are likely to occur. The primary author of Proverbs, Solomon, was the wisest man on earth at that time. His purpose was to convey his divinely inspired observations on the way human nature and God's universe work. He was saying that a given set of circumstances can be expected to produce certain consequences. Many people have taken numerous passages out of that context and made them to stand alone as promises from God. But how, then, can we explain why so many other proverbs do not inevitably prove accurate?

"Lazy hands make a man poor, but diligent hands bring wealth" (10:4).

"The fear of the LORD adds length to life, but the years of the wicked are cut short" (10:27).

"No harm befalls the righteous, but the wicked have their fill of trouble" (12:21).

"Plans fail for lack of counsel, but with many advisers they succeed" (15:22).

"Gray hair is a crown of splendor; it is attained by a righteous life" (16:31).

"The lot is cast into the lap, but its every decision is from the LORD" (16:33).

"A tyrannical ruler lacks judgment, but he who hates ill-gotten gain will enjoy a long life" (28:16).

I'm sure you can think of exceptions to the proverbs above. They appear to represent likelihoods rather than absolutes with God's personal guarantee attached.[5]

What, then, does Proverbs 22:6 tell us about parenting? It explains the parental responsibility to dedicate our children to God and train them in His ways.

In the original Hebrew, the phrase "in the way that he should go" reflects the thought that parents need to consider the particular child's stage of development and unique personality. The Amplified version says, "In keeping with his individual gift or bent." Rather than teaching that every child is to be responded to in the same way, this verse urges parents to train their child to love God and serve Him in light of the child's unique gifts and temperament.

Dr. Gleason Archer summarizes the parents' duties and their realistic expectations this way:

> This type of training implies a policy of treating children as even more important than one's own personal convenience or social life away from home. It means impressing on them that they are very important persons in their own right because they are loved by God, and because He has a wonderful and perfect plan for their lives. Parents who have faithfully followed these principles and practices in rearing their children may safely entrust them as adults to the keeping and guidance of God and feel no sense of personal guilt if the child later veers off course. They have done their best before God. The rest is up to each child himself.[6]

If you follow the advice in Proverbs 22:6, there's a good probability that children will either remain true to this instruction all their lives or return to God's teachings as they mature. Remember, though, that is only a probability, not a certainty. What's important is that you understand the uniqueness of each child's personality and adapt your responses to that uniqueness.

Many parents might continue to feel guilty when they read Proverbs 22:6 because they hear it saying they can expect their children to be converted only if they're perfect parents. But that line of thinking ignores the biblical passages assuring them that if they try to live godly lives, God will bless them.

God does not require or expect you to be perfect. He knows that's impossible. He asks only for your best effort.

I've heard parents quote other Scripture passages to extract a promise from God that their children will either remain true to Christian principles or return to the faith. Some people think, *If only I had more faith, my child would believe. After all, Jesus said, "Ask and it will be given to you; seek and you will find" (Luke 11:9). It's my fault, because I have so little faith.*[7]

Dr. James Kennedy described what he has seen:

> Some parents attempt to use "praise power" to manipulate or force God to touch their children's lives. They stand up in prayer meetings and say, with great emotion, "Father, I praise you because you have saved Susan. I praise you because she is a believer in your sight. I praise you because she is your daughter. Please manifest this truth in her life so I might praise you for that as well."
>
> Still other parents who are more traditional fall back upon the covenant promises of infant baptism. These parents maintain, "I had John baptized and made him a child of God. God never loses one of His children. He tells us this in the parable of the Good Shepherd. He must bring John to faith and repentance or He has broken His promise."
>
> Each of these approaches assumes that finite man can force the infinite God to act. This is a misunderstanding of the relationship between God and man. Ritualistic views of God teach that the divine Spirit must respond to certain words and actions of man just as members of the occult and priests of primitive

religions utter certain words and incantations to make their gods act. "Abracadabra and your wish is granted!"[8]

But biblical faith is much more complicated than that type of thinking! Our God is the personal Lord of the universe. He is working out His plan of redemption through Jesus Christ according to His perfect will. God is sovereign in our salvation, and He grants it according to His mercy upon whom He chooses (see Rom. 9-11; Eph. 1).

Our sovereign Lord can be touched by our prayers. He allows Himself to be influenced by them. But we can never force Him to act. We need to hope that He will act, yet always be ready to accept His decision with peace and submission.[9]

What a Parent Can Do

What can you do when you have an adolescent or young adult (as we did) who decides to go another direction with her life? For one thing, as with other crises, you are flung upon the grace and compassion of God to discover comfort for your pain and struggles. And in this process, there are steps you can take.

One step is to realize that adolescents and young adults must live with the consequences of their actions. Sin and rebellion always bring sorrow and hurt. When young adults do not immediately see consequences invade their lives as a result of their sin, it is simply God's mercy. We have all been mercifully delivered from the just results of our actions many times. It's always a relief when it happens, but we can't count on it. The apostle Paul addressed this issue when he wrote in Romans 2:4-6:

> Do you show contempt for the riches of his kindness, tolerance and patience, not realizing that God's kindness leads you toward repentance? But because of your stubbornness and your unrepentant heart, you are storing up wrath against yourself for the day of God's wrath, when his righteous judgment will be revealed. God "will give to each person according to what he has done."

Our children may suffer greatly, but the pain could be years in coming. We see this more and more, for example, with the AIDS epidemic. Yet rebellion is *their* choice, and the consequences are also theirs.

We need to wait with patience, which must come from the Lord. We'll suffer as we wait for our young adults to recognize their rebellion.

> *We'll suffer as we wait for our young adults to recognize their rebellion. But we must be there when they cry out for help and understanding.*

But we must be there when they cry out for help and understanding. They may not use words to express their needs. Listen for that silent cry, and cry with them. We did. You may have to wait years before you hear it or see any sign that their hardness is softening.

When you reenter their lives, do it slowly and with concern, not condemnation. Often they know the pain of guilt and conviction. They need to know you are there not to rescue but simply to receive, love, and help restore them.

Above all, keep the lines of communication open. Your letters and calls may go unanswered, but they won't be unseen or unheard. I worked recently with a parent, and over a period of weeks, six letters went unanswered. But the seventh one received an answer. Even when communication is strained or nonexistent, you can keep trying.

Use birthdays, holidays, and special occasions to send cards or make calls. If you're rejected, just keep reaching out.

Never give up praying. Ask God for another person to enter your children's lives and influence them in a godly direction. They can be swayed by peers or mentors. They may reveal themselves to others in a way they never can or will with parents.[10]

As a couple, we came to the conclusion that our role was to pray and attempt to love Sheryl unconditionally. We realized that others might have more influence than we did.

Joyce recalls her thoughts and concerns at that time:

My friend Fran and I felt led to pray and ask God to confront Sheryl and get her attention. We began daily to put her in God's hands, and we prayed that He would use whatever means necessary to bring her back to Himself. Sometimes God uses dramatic and painful events to draw us back. We discovered a pattern occurring after we prayed. In two or three days she would call—needy, hurting, and frightened over some incident.

Through the years of concern, Norm and I were able to sleep at night, even though we knew her chosen path could lead her into a great deal of trouble. We prayed for her protection and released her into God's hands.

A particular incident stands out in my mind. We were out of town, conducting a marriage seminar in the Grand Teton National Park. One night I awakened with a burden for Sheryl and just knew she had a great need at that time. All I could do was pray, knowing God knew what that need was. When we returned home, I casually mentioned what happened to Sheryl, and she asked about the day and time of my concern. When I told her, she thought for a moment, then turned very quiet and pale, inwardly recalling where she had been at that time. It was a moment when she realized that God still loved her and was trying to reach her.

We can remember other times when Christian women were able to sit and talk with Sheryl while she did their nails. (She's a manicurist.) Who will ever know how much Sheryl was influenced by others during that time? Keep praying for the recovery of your children and a spiritual healing in their lives.

The Rest of the Story

Here are three things you may need to remind yourself *not* to do: Don't pry, don't preach, and don't pressure a young adult who is either wandering or has returned.

When your adolescent or young adult child wanders, you will grieve. You *must* grieve over the hurt you're experiencing. After Sheryl told me what was happening in her life that day in my office, I was devastated. I grieved. Every morning for the next three weeks, as I did my morning workout on my exercise bike, I put on a recording by Dennis Agajanian titled "Rebel to the Wrong." And as I listened and rode, I wept. Joyce and I wondered when Sheryl's rebellion would end. We prayed and waited, waited and prayed.

After about three and a half years, we began to see indications of change in Sheryl's life. A friend asked her to accompany her to an Alcoholics Anonymous (AA) meeting for moral support. To Sheryl's surprise, as she heard the testimonies and information, she realized, *They're talking about me. I need to be here, too.* We never thought that one day we would be sitting in an AA meeting, listening to our daughter stand up and say, "Hi. My name is Sheryl. I'm an alcoholic," and then watch her receive her 30-day sobriety pin. But we've seen her conquer that problem.

A few months later, she had to enter the hospital for an operation on a herniated disk. While she was there, she told Joyce, "I just hope and pray that God will let me live through this so I can turn my life around and find my way back to Him."

A short while later, a Christian young man who is married to one of my relatives was visiting. As he talked with Sheryl, he asked her, "What are you going to do with your life?" That really set her to thinking.

That same weekend, we all went to church together at the First Presbyterian Church of Hollywood. Our pastor, Dr. Lloyd Ogilvie, was gone that Sunday, and Ralph Osborne was preaching. At the conclusion of services there, we provide an opportunity for people to come forward to

God can turn years of heartache with our children into occasions for great joy.

invite Jesus into their lives, to recommit their lives to the Lord, to receive prayer for healing, and so on. I will never forget sitting in the silence of that moment and then hearing a quiet voice in my ear say, "Daddy, will you walk up there with me?"

With tears in my eyes, I followed her to the front of the church and had the privilege of seeing her kneel there, talk with an elder, and then recommit her life to Jesus Christ. It was a commitment that included a dramatic turnaround in her total life-style.

Later that day, Sheryl said, "Daddy, I was doing fine emotionally until

I looked at you and saw that you were losing it, and then I lost control and cried, too." We both laughed at her comment, realizing we were crying tears of joy. Joyce and I are so thankful that God can turn years of heartache with our children into occasions for great joy.

You may not be there yet. Your child may still be wandering. It may seem like forever. And for some, it could be. Sometimes parents won't see the wandering child return. But never, never give up hope. Keep praying. And perhaps for you, as it happened for us, the parable of the prodigal in Luke 15 will take on more significance. Actually, we can all relate to that story, because in one way or another, aren't we all prodigals? It's just that some of us are more obvious than others.

Keep Dreaming

Let me conclude this chapter on a positive note as a means of encouragement. The joyful occasions that you thought may have been lost forever can become a reality.

I've been talking about the shattering of our dreams for our children. There's nothing wrong with dreams—as long as they are realistic and have not been set in concrete. We naturally want our children to be a reflection of our beliefs, values, and standards.

I had high hopes for our daughter's academic success. I now understand the reasons for my expectations much better than I did then. When I realized Matthew would never progress much beyond a two-year-old mentally, my hopes for Sheryl and her academic pursuits increased dramatically. I assumed she would attend and complete college. After all, since I had completed college and two graduate programs, why wouldn't Sheryl follow that same path?

But those were my dreams, not hers. Sheryl quit college after one year and became a licensed manicurist in a nail salon. Her career choice wasn't what I would have chosen, but I was not the one to choose. And then she began to excel in her field. She applied her God-given artistic talent to her work by doing nail art—painting miniature scenes on the nails of her customers.

Sheryl learned most of what she did on her own, without benefit of lessons. She would create a new idea and never stop to think it couldn't be accomplished. She also learned the art of air brushing on her own and even designed some new nail styles. Her skill developed to the point that she won several national competitions in this field, taught for a major nail company, and opened her own nail salon in which she did her own interior decorating. Our daughter eventually built one of the finest businesses in this field in her city.

Another joyful occasion was seeing our daughter become engaged to a fine Christian man. Who would have thought that two years after walking her down the aisle to recommit her life to the Lord, I would have the privilege of escorting her down the aisle to be married? And during the time of wedding preparations, some memorable events occurred.

The wedding day itself was a high point in my life. I was concerned about holding myself together during the ceremony, but that went well. However, two days later, while I was watching the wedding video, all the feelings burst to the surface.

Another event at that time was very special for us as parents. Prior to her wedding day, Sheryl talked to us about Matthew, who was 22 years old at the time. "I know Matthew won't be able to come to the ceremony," she said, "but I would still like him to be a part of my wedding. The next time he's home for a visit, could we rent a tuxedo for him so he and I can be photographed together?"

Needless to say, her request brought deep joy to us. Due to many factors, we were unable to fulfill her request, but at that time it appeared to be all right. Sheryl's thoughtful offer was very meaningful to us and remains a precious memory. Now that Matthew is gone (see chapter 3), it's one of those events we wish had happened.

During more than 25 years of premarital counseling, I have always requested that the parents of the engaged couple write a letter to their prospective son- or daughter-in-law, welcoming him or her into their family. I've heard hundreds of those letters read in my office. For years we looked forward to writing such a letter to Sheryl's future husband. I was glad when Bill and Sheryl's counselor, who is a good friend of mine, requested that Joyce and I write a letter of welcome to Bill, which we did.

We also wanted to write a letter to Sheryl. We wanted to express in a special way our love for her and our happiness for her future with Bill. It was our way of releasing her to the man God had brought into her life.

Following the counselor's instructions, we mailed our letter for Bill to the counselor and included our letter to Sheryl. When their counseling session came, he gave Bill our welcoming letter. Then he said to Sheryl, "There's an additional letter here for you, Sheryl, from your parents. But instead of giving this to you to read, let me suggest that you take it home and ask your father to read it to you."

When she came home with that request, I wasn't ready for it. Yet, knowing her counselor as I do, I shouldn't have been surprised.

I waited for three days so we could all sit down together as I read Sheryl that letter from Joyce and me. I'm so glad we were asked to do so. It was such a special time. With Sheryl's permission, we want to share the letter with you:

Dear Sheryl,

You probably didn't expect to receive a letter from us at this time, but we have always wanted to write a letter to our about-to-be-married daughter. And that time is here—finally!

For years we have prayed for your choice of the man with whom you will spend the rest of your life. Patience does have its rewards, doesn't it?

Sheryl, our desire for you is that you have a marriage which is fulfilling, satisfying, and glorifying to God. You, as a woman, have so much to offer. You have God-given talents and abilities which, with each year of your life, emerge more and more. You have a sensitivity and love to give Bill that will enhance your marriage.

We know there are times when you get down on yourself and feel discouraged. Never give up on yourself. God never has, nor will, and we never have, nor will. Treat yourself with the respect that God has for you. Allow Him to enable you to continue to develop now as a married woman. Jesus Christ has started a new work in you, and He will bring it to completion.

Sheryl, you have brought so much delight and joy into our lives, and we thank God that you have been our daughter for all these years. We have all grown together through learning to accept one another and through some difficult times of hurt and pain. That's life! But because of Jesus Christ, we all learn through those hard times.

We look forward to becoming parents of a married daughter. Mrs. Bill Macauley: doesn't that have a great sound!

Sheryl, thank you for how you have enriched our lives. Thank you for who you are.

We love you,
Mom and Dad[11]

⁓Three⁓

The Homegoing

IN the spring of 1989, after Matthew had been at the home about ten years, he went through a graduation program, complete with cap and gown, at the school he attended. He was 21 years old, and with his ambling gait and facial expression, he appeared even more physically disabled. His vocabulary consisted of only eight or ten words, and we never knew if he understood the meaning of even those few words.

We had developed a ritual of taking Matthew to Knott's Berry Farm for his birthday each year. We would go on two or three of the simple rides and walk him around to see the animals. Sometimes he appeared to enjoy the experience, but often he gave little or no response. We didn't really know if he liked or even noticed what was going on. But that was all right. One lesson we learned was that when you do something for another person, you don't always have to get a response. You do it regardless of whether it's ever acknowledged.

One day when we stopped by to visit, we took Matthew out to eat at a restaurant near Salem Home. During lunch, we had disaster after disaster. First, we were in a booth enclosed by wood partitions and glassed in just above our heads. The wood acted like an amplifying device. Matthew's food was too spicy, and we had to place another order. (One thing about Matthew—he did not like to wait for his food.)

He had downed one glass of milk already, so we ordered another. It came, but we didn't want him to drink it too soon, so we put it on the other side of the table. He sat there staring at the milk for the longest time, and then he slowly rose, leaned over the table, and grasped the glass with both hands as though he was going to pull it toward him.

With a cry, both Joyce and I grabbed the milk, and a giant tug-of-war developed, with the glass going nowhere. Seated just behind us was a well-dressed, dignified-looking couple, and in our minds, the worst nightmare was beginning to form. We could just envision Matthew winning the contest and heaving that heavy glass of milk over his head, through the glass, and onto the couple. We held on even tighter!

All of a sudden, it seemed as though Matthew decided, "All right, if it's not coming to me, I'll go to it." He rose up and leaned over the table, put his mouth on the glass, and began to drink while it was stationary on the table. He slurped up quite a bit and left a ring of milk around his mouth. With that, he seemed to be satisfied and sat down. We breathed a sigh of relief. We completed the meal and left the restaurant with an abundance of food scattered over the table, the bench, and the floor. When Matthew ate out, he enjoyed himself.

A Serious Condition

As we took Matthew back to Salem that day, he began to spit up his food. We had heard about the problem, but now we saw it for the first time.

Joyce tells what happened next:

When we arrived back at Salem, I talked to the staff about his regurgitation of some of his meal and then seeming to play with it. It was both a medical condition and a self-stimulating behavior. The problem continued, and we were able to observe it more. The Salem and school staffs had tried many different ways to stop the repetitive behavior, but nothing seemed to work.

In the fall of 1989, Norm and I returned home from conducting a marriage seminar, and when we saw Matthew, we were shocked. He had lost 13 pounds, and he was thin to begin with. Now he was down to 91 pounds. From that time on, the staff at Salem and the doctors treated the problem as a serious medical disorder—reflux esophagitis—a burning of the lining of the esophagus.

A new sense of urgency arose. Something had to be done, and the frustration of not being able to communicate with him about his destructive habit left us feeling helpless once again. He couldn't tell us about the discomfort and pain he surely was experiencing. (That's often the case with a disabled child.)

The specialist said there were medications to try but that they didn't always work. And in that case, surgery might be necessary.

Although the medical staff did all they could, the medication didn't work. It was obvious that surgery would have to be done. An operation on the valve between the esophagus and the stomach that controlled the regurgitation response was required. Even with a fine medical staff, we realized we could ultimately depend only on our Lord. Thus, we moved ahead with plans for the operation, and both of us, as well as friends, donated blood for the pending surgery.

The Sunday before surgery was scheduled, during worship at our church, we sang the hymn "Holy, Holy, Holy." Two words stood out to me— *merciful* and *mighty.* God is merciful and mighty! Matthew was entirely in God's hands, and I was certain He would be merciful when it came to our precious young son. We also knew that God is mighty and powerful, and nothing is too difficult for Him.

The day of surgery came, and Matthew was very bright and having a wonderful morning. As we drove to the hospital, he heard a siren, and he threw back his head and laughed hilariously. To him, sirens were a happy, delightful sound. That was the last time I heard him laugh with glee, but I treasure the memory of those times of laughter over the years. As we sat in the waiting room, a close friend arrived to spend time and pray with us. We were still there in the late afternoon when all of a sudden, the room began to vibrate and then shake as a result of the Upland earthquake centered just 25 miles away.

The operation appeared to go all right, although the esophagus was thin as tissue paper from the effect of the stomach acids. It was torn during the surgery, but that was repaired. During the week of hospitalization, we were thankful for the competent doctors and nurses God had provided.

> *I knew in my heart that Matthew's life was in the balance, and I marveled at the security we have in God's love.*

In the first few days after surgery, Matthew suffered complications, and infection set in. We alternated staying at motels near the hospital and driving home. Norm would go to the counseling center during the day and return to the hospital later. He gave me emotional support and understood that I needed to be there at Matthew's bedside.

Daily, I prayed on the phone with my best friend. After many years of praying with her, it was a comfortable, natural way to weather a crisis. We were also sustained by the prayers of Matthew's sister, his grandmothers, and our other friends.

One beautiful morning, as I drove to the hospital, this Scripture came on the radio: "For I am convinced that neither death, nor life, nor angels, nor principalities, nor things present, nor things to come, nor powers, nor height, nor depth, nor any other created thing, shall be able to separate us from the love of God, which is in Christ Jesus our Lord" (Rom. 8:38-39, NASB). The phrase "death, nor life" seemed to stand out. I knew in my heart that Matthew's life was in the balance, and I marveled at the security we have in God's love.

Early on, the nurses seemed relieved that I was there, and they asked me questions since they couldn't communicate with Matthew. They let me know my presence was needed. I felt that being his mother was a special privilege. Their main question was, "How does he show he's in pain?" They needed to know when to give him medication. I was eager to help in any way I could, but I was at a loss to answer that question. (They had no choice but to just medicate him at regular intervals.)

As I visited each day, our time together was special. I patted Matthew's hand and talked to him in simple, loving words. He didn't reach out and respond, but his eyes followed me as I moved about the room. It was touching to see him content and peaceful, even during his times of discomfort.

I was aware of God's presence through the days at the hospital. I was reassured that He was in control, and I had a sense of being uplifted by the prayers of family and friends. I was even able to reach out to a family dealing with their son's tragic motorcycle accident, which had caused massive trauma to his head.

After a week, additional surgery was performed. Following the operation, Matthew stayed in the intensive care unit. He was heavily sedated and unconscious. There were eight tubes in him, and he was constantly on a ventilator. He developed adult respiratory disorder syndrome. We were hopeful when the fever dropped and his blood pressure stabilized, but in several days we could see that he was not responding. The doctors felt he was in the Lord's hands. We prayed at his bedside for the Lord's will to be done.

Matthew Goes Home

We had stayed at our home the night of March 14 instead of at a motel near the Loma Linda Hospital. I woke up at 4:00 A.M. with the feeling that Matthew was worse. I called the hospital, and the staff confirmed my fears. They had gone to full power on the ventilator. Around 7:00 that morning, as we were getting ready for the day, we received a phone call. It was one of the medical staff, and he said, "We would like you to come to the hospital as soon as possible." His request didn't need any amplification.

Fortunately, we were able to speed through the traffic those 60 miles to the hospital. Both of us were aware that it could be Matthew's final hour. We had not seen any response from him for days.

Norm and I walked into the room, and the doctors told us that Matthew's lungs and heart were failing and would probably stop in about an hour. My initial response, which might surprise you if you've never had a loved one suffer and die, was profound joy. I was truly happy for him. I said, "Oh, he'll be in the presence of the Lord this day!" I knew he would be finished with the struggles of this world, totally healed, and finally out of pain.

We both felt that way. But we also felt helpless since there was nothing anyone could do to make Matthew well again. As much as we knew he was going to a far better place, we also knew we were facing the greatest loss of our lives.

We said good-bye to Matthew, and I prayed at his bedside, thanking the Lord for our precious child and for His provision of eternal life. As we stood there, we saw Matthew's pulse rate decline ten beats. We felt as though we were giving him back to God and saying, "He's Yours. Have Your perfect will with him." We believed God had something better for him.

Matthew's decreasing vital signs confirmed the reality that he was going to die soon. The doctors said we could stay there or wait in a family room, and we chose the latter. Within an hour, the doctors came to tell us Matthew had died. We cried and talked with them. God was truly loving and merciful when He took Matthew home that day, and we bowed to His perfect will. Perhaps others won't understand our mixture of feelings, but that's all right. We felt at peace.

I learned a lot about Norm from our son's death. It revealed to me his depth of emotion, love, and caring. I was amazed at how tender his feelings were and how easily the tears came for him. We were more aware of our oneness as we shared our grief and discussed how the Lord had gently prepared us for this time. Tears also have been a friend for me. Often they will come during a worship experience, and I become aware of the Holy Spirit's comfort and healing in my heart. They also come at some of the most unexpected moments.

The next few days were filled with arrangements for the funeral and people calling and coming by to express their concern. The morning of the service seemed to be going fairly well until Sheryl brought her own creative arrangement of flowers in a basket. She had also put in a small stuffed toy, along with our favorite picture of the two of them together. Seeing that triggered a torrent of tears that seemed to go on and on. But every time we cried, we realized we needed to and that we were using one of God's gifts.

The service was inspiring, encouraging, and comforting. Our pastor, Dr. Lloyd Ogilvie, took several minutes to read passages from God's Word, and it struck us anew how much comfort there is in simply hearing it.

He closed the service with the following words:

> "And Jesus said except you become as a little child you cannot enter the kingdom of heaven." We meet together with the assurance that Matthew, though childlike in spirit, knew that relationship with Jesus Christ by Christ's election and love and acceptance that made his death but a transition into the midst of living. And as the fellowship of faith this afternoon, we claim what Paul has said, "Our bodies are sown in weakness but raised in power." That is now true for Matthew. Handicapped? I would say "handicapable," for most of the attributes that we develop in life keep us *from* rather than bring us *to* the Father. The simple trust that we knew as a child is often blighted by the growth of our theories, our supposed maturity. Over and over again every day of our lives, we must become a child again and run to our Father and know His love and His forgiveness.
>
> You can just imagine that the company of heaven today has a new voice. It's Matthew's voice singing with the angels and archangels around the throne of God, whole, complete in Christ. A miracle? Oh yes. But God's miracle is offered to each of us this afternoon. If this were our day, could we run to our Father with that same kind of trust and know for sure that we were going to spend eternity with Him?

Oh, Matthew taught his family so much. And he continues teaching here today. But there's nothing we can do to achieve our righteousness with God. There's not one thing that we can say or accomplish or write or speak that will make God love us any more than He does right now. That's what Matthew taught and teaches by his life. So much of our time is spent trying to accomplish those things that we think will make God take notice of us. But He loves us just as we are, as He loved Matthew.

One of my favorite stories that I think of often is of that semaphore message that was sent about Wellington's battle at Waterloo. You remember. It was interrupted halfway through when the clouds came down over the English Channel. The semaphore worded it out, "Wellington defeated . . .," and then the fog came down and the rest of the message didn't reach England for 48 hours. When the fog lifted, the semaphore completed the message, "Wellington defeated the enemy."

Our faith in Christ is that Matthew defeated all of the enemies—the enemies of disabilities, of incompleteness, and death. And his voice now has not just eight to ten words but a thousand tongues to sing Christ's praise, and in that we rejoice. Hallelujah, hallelujah, hallelujah.

We so appreciated Dr. Ogilvie's sermon and his abundant use of Scripture for the strength they gave us. Following the message, a friend and classmate from Westmont, Paul Sandberg, concluded the service by singing "No More Night." The words of one portion of this song of hope and triumph are, "No more night, no more pain, no more tears, never crying again. Praises to the great I Am, we will live in the light of the risen Lamb."[1]

Other Losses

Losing Matthew was a tremendous blow in and of itself. But like any major loss, it also caused a number of additional, or secondary, losses. The routine we had followed for years was gone forever. We would no longer look through catalogs to select his special sleepwear. We wouldn't have the special weekends in which he would come home and stay overnight, nor would we be able to stop by Salem Home to take him out to eat. Instead, we would drive past where he used to live and keep traveling along the freeway.

We faced future losses as well. Matthew would no longer be at home on Thanksgiving or Christmas, nor would we take him to Knott's Berry Farm for his birthday. Those losses we could anticipate, but each week brought others we didn't expect. (If he had been living at home, there would have been daily losses.) We couldn't call Salem anymore to see how he was doing, a topic of our conversation was gone, and certain phrases or expressions we would say to him would no longer be expressed.

Sometimes the way we discovered the other losses was surprising. Eight months after Matthew died, we acquired a dog. For years we had raised shelties, but now we selected a golden retriever puppy that we named Sheffield. One day I walked by the kitchen, and through the door, I heard Joyce saying something to Sheffield that stopped me in my tracks. I opened the door and asked, "Joyce, what did you just say to Sheff?"

She said, "Oh, I was just saying, 'Hey, you,' while I was playing with him."

Then it dawned on her, as it had on me, that she had frequently used that expression when talking to Matthew. We hadn't heard it for such a long time, and we felt his loss again.

Another day, we took the dog to the vet for shots and a checkup. Joyce wrapped Sheffield in a large towel and held him on her lap as we drove. Halfway there, she began crying, and I looked over and asked what was wrong. "I just realized this is the same towel I always used with Matthew when I bathed him at home, and that I wouldn't be using this with him anymore," she said. "I want to save this towel and remember those happy bubble baths." Once again, we felt the intrusion of a loss.

A friend who knew the story of Matthew and how we were prepared for his arrival and subsequent move to Salem Home asked me, "Norm, God prepared you for Matthew's coming and then release to the home, but how did He prepare you for his death?" I was thrown a bit by the question, and at the moment I couldn't come up with an answer. But later, as I reflected on the question, it became clear. Over the six or seven years prior to Matthew's death, I had been teaching and writing more and more in the area of crisis counseling and grief recovery. All that preparation helped us accept what we were experiencing and feeling during our loss. Once again, we could see God's providential working in our lives.

God's Grace

Through Matthew's death, we learned in a new way about the grace of God. It came from the response of friends, people we knew, and others we hadn't even met. We learned about the value of their words, their silent presence, and their phone calls that continued not just for a few weeks but for years. We weren't forgotten, nor was Matthew. When I talked about the impact of his life on us as individuals and on our marriage, as I had done for years, I had a new segment of his story to relate. And again, we have seen how God has used that aspect of his life to minister to others. It seems we now have a new ministry to parents who have lost a child in death. That's how God takes the upsets in our lives and gives them deeper significance.

Through Matthew's death, we learned in a new way about the grace of God.

Of the many responses we received, we would like to share two with you. A few days after the memorial service, I received a note in the mail with an original psalm. It was written by one of my former seminary students who is now a professor in the department of Christian education at Talbot Graduate School of Theology, where I was his professor. He said he had "dabbled a bit in creative writing" and wanted to share his concern with us.

This is what he sent, which we reprint with his permission:

A Psalm about the Loss of Treasure

LORD, you told us not to lay up for ourselves
treasure on earth.
You said moths and rust would corrupt

and thieves would break in and steal it.
You told us, LORD, to lay up our treasures in heaven.
You promised, LORD,
that moths and rust wouldn't corrupt those
and You promised, LORD,
that thieves couldn't steal it either.

Well, that's what they did, LORD.
That's what my friends did.
My friends Norm and Joyce laid up their treasure in heaven.
Yes, they did.
That treasure which You had given them so many years ago
now.
That treasure which they knew early
was not perfect.
That treasure which would need so much from them;
but was no less treasure just the same.
They called the treasure Matthew, and they loved him;
oh, how they loved him!

In just a small collection of minutes they knew something was
seriously wrong.
Matthew was not like other Matthews, or Andrews,
or treasures by any other names.
Matthew was different, and they came to even
love the difference in their treasure.

Now, LORD, now . . . . What about your promise?
You promised thieves wouldn't steal.
I and my friends believed your promise.
But their treasure is taken from them.
Isn't that stealing?

OK. You took the treasure.
And I and my friends don't really know why.
But, You did and maybe one day I can say,

"That's OK."
But right now, I can't.
I wonder if my friends can say that.
I don't know, but if they can, they know you
better than I do, I guess.

But what of their treasure, Matthew?
Is he running and playing in your heaven today?
Can he speak and say things like
"ice cream" and "chocolate candy" and "going fishing"?
Things
he could never say to Norm and Joyce?
Can he laugh and hug and squeal and say
"I love you, Mom!"
Maybe my friends are really gonna like what
you've done with their treasure.
Maybe just "one world away"
they're gonna see their treasure again
and say, "Boy, that's great!"
Maybe they are beginning even now to understand
that Matthew is really YOUR treasure.
I don't understand that exactly,
but maybe my friends do.

Help them, LORD!
Please be the things to them I wish I could be;
but can't.
Maybe you can say to Joyce,
"I love you, Mom,"
and she'll understand.
Maybe you can say to Norm,
"Let's go fishing, Dad,"
and he'll know what that means.

Thank you, LORD, for understanding me
and for comforting my friends.

I love you—
and I know they do too.[2]

Seven months later, I received the following letter from someone I had never met. Once again, Joyce and I were amazed by the depth of concern and compassion that exists with God's people:

> Three weeks ago, I received my *Focus on the Family* magazine that spoke of your appearance on Dr. Dobson's program. The subject of the show was, as you know, about the passing of a mentally handicapped child, your son, Matthew. My son Michael went home to be with the Lord on August 21, 1990. He is so missed, yet I do know he is in the arms of the Master. I do not regret my son's birth nor his passing, because both those events were a beginning and a healing. I have problems with the 14 years that Mike wasn't normal.
>
> Michael was damaged during a difficult labor at Balboa Hospital. The doctors at that time couldn't tell us anything regarding Mike's future. At three weeks, he arrested and was rushed to the nearest Navy clinic, and from there was taken to Sharp Hospital in San Diego. The Navy clinic didn't have an oxygen mask small enough to fit an infant, so Mike had to make the 15-mile trip via mouth to mouth. His blood gases were below 5, and later a doctor told me if he had been an adult he would have been declared dead on arrival. Yet, with babies they apply different criteria for emergencies.
>
> Michael was in the hospital for 2 months and discharged. One doctor told me he couldn't predict Michael's future—it was his job to save his life. I was a young mother, happily married (and still married) to a young Marine. Shawn and I took home a very spoiled little boy that scared us to death. The doctors told me to throw out my baby books because Michael wouldn't progress at the rate of a normal child. Michael didn't hold up his head without support and never sucked his thumb, held a toy, rolled over, spoke, crawled, or sat up. Yet he was ours, and we loved him. No one could tell us anything. Michael would be what

God wanted, and why would God give two pretty good Christians a damaged baby? The healing or mending was coming. My little boy would always be a baby, never progressing past three weeks.

One day, while talking with my older brother, I casually mentioned that God had given us Michael for a purpose, and I just needed to discover what it was. My brother looked at me and said, "Cat, God didn't damage Michael; he was damaged because his birth was mishandled. I do not have a problem with you looking for God's direction regarding Michael, but I do have a problem with you blaming God."

At that moment, I realized that God's intention is for all mothers and fathers to have perfect babies. Sin made the intentions or results different or difficult. My baby hadn't done anything to warrant this, yet mankind has asked the question "Why?" The blind man at the gate was the source of the question, "Why is he this way?" To show the glory of God this day! My son touched every life he came upon. Nobody wasn't moved by this little boy. He made you slow down.

Michael made it possible for Shawn and I to accept our son Nathan. Nate was born December 20, 1978. He had a virus before birth and has severe cerebral palsy and is mentally retarded. He is my happy, "merry" baby. Nate was followed four years later by Emily—she is my child of faith. Although neither Michael nor Nathan have a genetic problem, I do not believe in abortion and knew that if the problem could be inherited, I just wouldn't have any more children. But life is too special for me to decide who lives and who doesn't. The ability to give life is wonderful and special. God gave life to Adam. That puts a level of importance on this decision that isn't mine to make. Life must be protected.

Once, at a women's meeting, a woman said to me, "With your children, you should be pro-choice. Then your family wouldn't be suffering."

I looked at her and said, "Where do we draw the line? Retarded children, physically handicapped, disfigured?" Maybe someone would decide *she* didn't fit the bill. She was momentarily silent.

I have talked your ear off—and thank you for your time. Michael has been home for two months. Heaven is very lucky. I can't honestly say I am glad he is gone. I miss him so much. I would love to kiss his fingers and forehead, look into his brown eyes. Yet I am glad he can walk and talk. I would love to have heard his voice. Michael was a presence in our home. Just today I told my mother, to the world it is as if Mike didn't exist, but to me and his father, sister, and family, we have a hole that needs to be filled. God has been good. In Psalm 27:1, He speaks to me, "The Lord is my light—the Lord is my strength."[3]

Need we say any more?

ᗑFourᗒ
Handling the News of Loss

Explaining the feeling of loss to someone who hasn't been there is difficult. There's nothing like it. Perhaps the word *devastation* best describes it. Remember the TV pictures of the Los Angeles riots in 1992? As the rioting subsided and a sense of calm settled over the city, people returned to see what had once been their homes and stores. The look on their faces told the story as they gazed at the devastation.

During the same year, scenes of devastation appeared again and again, only this time because of Hurricanes Andrew and Iniki. We watched the winds increase until they were ripping chunks from roofs and tearing houses apart piece by piece. After the storms passed and the winds subsided, an eerie silence settled over the hard-hit areas. People made their way through the debris-filled streets until they found the places where they used to live. It was sad to see them picking through the remnants, looking for something that could be salvaged and restored.

At times you could see a glimmer of hope as they found something important to them. The next moment, the despair and anger returned when what they held fell apart in their hands. They searched through pile after pile of rubble, eventually finding a few items that, to us, wouldn't seem significant but were all they had left. What might not have had much meaning before took on a whole new perspective.

In the face of such loss, values change. Life-styles are altered. Expectations once held so dear undergo radical surgery. The survivors wonder what will happen to them, how they'll make it. Of course, the questions can't be answered, because no one knows the future.

When you suffer a serious loss, the well-meaning platitudes of others sound empty and insensitive and sometimes anger you. How do they

You keep returning to these questions: "Why? Why me? Why us? Why now?"

know what will happen? Besides, you're numb. You're in shock. The loss wasn't expected. It's not what you wanted. How dare it invade your life and upset everything!

You keep returning to these questions: "Why? Why me? Why us? Why now?" In time, as the shock diminishes, you wonder how you'll survive, because you're exhausted from continually riding an emotional roller coaster. Eventually, the questions turn to "What am I going to do? How will we make it through this? What do we have to do to survive?" When people were interviewed following the riots and hurricanes, one after another asked those same questions, and their faces reflected the same shock and grief.

The reaction of the riot and hurricane victims is very similar to the response of parents who have been told that their child was born with a disability, has a terminal illness, is involved in drugs, has lost his hearing in an accident, or will die in the next hour. The parents' response could be more intense, however, because the tragedy involves a person, a beloved child. (Though I'm focusing on the property loss from the riots and hurricanes, I know many lives were lost as well.)

Some homes and stores can be rebuilt. Others will remain as they were, reflecting the destruction for years to come. The loss of dreams, heirlooms, and economic security can be overwhelming. But in a riot or hurricane, you don't feel so alone, because others around you are going through the same experience. When something happens to your child in otherwise normal times, however, you feel isolated. Life is going on for everyone around you. It still seems routine for them. But for you it has stopped.

When you receive the news of your loss, you are jerked from the safe, familiar routine of your life into the threatening and unfamiliar. The uncertainties will keep you off balance. After the shock subsides, your companions will be fear, anger, anxiety, sadness, depression, denial, hysteria, and guilt.

The Initial Stage: Shock

The initial response of shock and its accompanying numbness can be seen as a gift of God, for He created us to react in this protective way. Shock gives us time to withdraw from the sharpness of the pain. Our shock turns into an emotional anesthesia that helps us develop the coping mechanisms we need to handle the news and survive the assault. This is healthy; it's actually the first stage in the healing process.

I've talked with parents who lived with their shock and numbness for just a day; others have stayed in that stage for weeks or even months. If a normal child was injured and became disabled, or if he appeared normal and then was diagnosed as having a disability, parents may stay longer in this stage. Sometimes one parent moves on but the other gets stuck. I worked with one mother who remained caught in this stage for more than two years.

If shock persists for several days or weeks, it may become an unwelcome visitor and lose its value. Some parents hang on to numbness as a way of walling themselves off from the pain that is pushing to penetrate again and their inner grief that is struggling to burst out. At the time, it may seem safe and comfortable to keep all those growing emotions buried. After all, such intense feelings hurt and disrupt lives. Unless parents allow them to rise above the numbness and face them squarely, however, they will never move beyond grief. They'll never function fully again. They'll never find acceptable answers. And those who try to keep the problem a secret or lessen its reality will have the most difficulty.

When water is frozen, the molecules actually expand with enough power to burst pipes wide open. So when we lock up a mountain cabin for the winter, we must drain all the water from the pipes if we want them to function properly the next spring. And like frozen water molecules, frozen emotions take on a power out of proportion to their original nature. During grief, it's important to keep the channels open for the feelings to flow when they need to.

Some of us release our feelings verbally because that's what we know best. Others of us find alternative means. We shouldn't compare ourselves with others and say one way of release is the only way or the best way. You may spend a great deal of time working in your yard or running, but you don't talk about your loss. Others may be concerned that you're not dealing with your loss, but you may be doing it in your own way. Eventually, you will benefit by verbalizing your feelings.

People use many unique ways of coping with loss. A man lived near his parents on an adjacent farm. One night, the home in which he was born and raised burned to the ground with his father inside. The man's response to the tragedy startled other family members. He remained silent while they all wept and talked about the loss. Then he borrowed a bulldozer and proceeded to bulldoze the charred remains of the house.

Rain had stopped the fire, and that was his expression of burying his father. He worked for hours, not even stopping for meals or rest. When darkness came, he ignored the requests of family members to stop for the night. He continued to bulldoze the remains back and forth, again and again.

For most of their lives, the farmer and his father had worked together in the fields. They didn't talk much or share feelings. But theirs was a close, caring relationship.

You and I may grieve with tears, but that man grieved with his borrowed bulldozer. It was his personal expression of words and tears. He cried by working the land over and over until nothing was visible. He gave his father and the home a proper burial—but in his own way. The land, which in a sense was his father's cemetery, was now ready to be farmed, and he would do it. If you asked the man why he did it, he couldn't give you an answer. He didn't know why, but he did something with his grief, and it was probably the best thing he could have done.

What do you need during the initial phase of a loss? You need to accept your feelings. You need an environment that helps your grieving and hurts to heal. Avoid people who are full of advice and say "I told you so" or "Spiritual Christians get over their hurt sooner than others."

Those who search out help immediately will find comfort and will more than likely become survivors. But you must grieve first. It's inevitable in order to go on. I didn't fully realize that when I received the

You must acknowledge grief and allow it to surface.

news about Matthew. All I knew was that it hurt, my life was disrupted, and I didn't feel in control anymore.

We usually associate grief with death, but there's grief with any loss. And when you have a disabled, injured, or wayward child, you don't just grieve for a while and then come out of it to find it's all over. It's more like living with a constant low-grade fever and now and then taking a vacation from it. This coming and going throughout the life of the experience will vary with every person.

You must acknowledge grief and allow it to surface. When it isn't acknowledged, full acceptance of and adjustment to the situation become even more difficult than usual. That's a tragedy not only for you, but for your child as well.

There's nothing heroic or noble about grief. It's painful. It's work. It's a lingering process. But it is necessary for all kinds of loss. It has been labeled everything from intense mental anguish to acute sorrow to deep remorse.

Emotions Out of Control

Numerous emotions involved in the grief process seem out of control and often appear in conflict with one another. With each loss come bitterness, emptiness, apathy, love, anger, guilt, sadness, fear, self-pity, and helplessness. These feelings

usher in the emotional freeze that covers solid ground with ice, making movement in any direction seem precarious and dangerous. Growth is hidden, progress seems blocked, and one bleakly speculates that just because the crocuses made it through the snow last year is no reason to believe they can do it again this year. It's not a pretty picture.[1]

Seasons of depression, anger, calm, fear, and, eventually, hope will come, but they don't follow one another progressively. They overlap and are often jumbled together. Just when you think you're over one, it comes bursting through your door again. You finally smile, but then the tears return. You laugh, but the cloud of depression drifts in once again. This is normal. This is necessary. This is healing.

The griever's suffering is never constant. Waves of pain alternate with lulls of momentary rest. Initially, of course, in acute grief situations, the waves are intense and frequent. Gradually, as you're healed, the waves are less intense, less prolonged, and less frequent.

We can almost imagine the wave patterns charted on a graph, like radio waves. Each peak represents a mountain of pain, each valley a restful lull. Initially, the peaks are high and long, the valleys are narrow and short, and the frequency is high. Slowly, the peaks mellow, the valleys lengthen, and the frequency decreases.

Gradually, ever so gradually, the storm quiets. Yet months and years later, an isolated wave can still come crashing ashore. On sentimental holidays, for example, the memories of lost loved ones are often raw. "Every Christmas," says a widowed, middle-aged woman, "after all the busyness is over, I sit down and have a good cry." Periodically, an isolated wave of grief washes against the shore of one's soul.[2]

Some parents grieve on each birthday of their disabled child, both for themselves and for the child. All three of them miss what could have been.

When grief hits, it affects you psychologically through your feelings, thoughts, and attitudes. It affects you socially as you interact with others. It affects you physically in your health and in bodily symptoms.

Grief encompasses several changes. It appears differently at various times, and it flits in and out of your life. It is not an abnormal response. In fact, just the opposite is true. The absence of grief is abnormal. Grief is your personal experience. Your loss does not have to be accepted or validated by others for you to experience and express grief.[3]

Why grief? Why do you have to go through this experience? Grief responses express basically three things:

1. Through grief, you express your feelings about your loss, and there are many.

2. Through grief, you express your protest at the loss, as well as your desire to change what happened and have it not be true.

3. Through grief, you express the effects you have experienced from the devastating impact of the loss.[4]

Grief includes that feeling of sadness and depression. Sometimes that's when your pain is most intense, for there's no anxiety or anger to cover it. Your companion will be tears now. And I hope they will be on the outside. Too many people—especially men—can cry only on the inside.

The problem with tears is that you never know when they'll emerge. As many have said, when you experience a major loss, you end up being ambushed by grief. I understand that statement far better since Matthew's death. I never know what will trigger tears again.

Uninvited Visitors

One of your uninvited visitors at this time will be guilt. It's a very normal response when you have a child who is disabled or drifting, or even when you lose a child to death. It's so easy to slip into a pattern of thinking that throws the fault at your feet, and you end up believing the problem is due to some failure on your part. Unfortunately, some cultures promote this type of thinking.

Guilty feelings generate more and more pain. Sometimes the parents *did* cause a child's problem. I've seen children disabled because of the mother's alcohol use during pregnancy, a parent's failure to strap the child in a car seat, or parental abuse or neglect. But even justifiable guilt, after it has been acknowledged and experienced, cannot be held onto. Immersing yourself in guilt doesn't resolve the problem; it only compounds it. It generates more pain for you, the child, and everyone else in the family. Guilt needs to be relinquished.

Rejection will creep into your life as well. Accepting what has happened can be difficult, as can accepting the child, whether the problem is a disability or the denouncing of your teaching and values. I've seen some situations where the rejection is permanent. Some parents become "token" moms and dads, providing the physical necessities of life, yet the child feels rejected because of the emotional starvation. The rejection occurs as the parents use excessive denial, numbness, or grief to create an ongoing distance between themselves and their child.

Whenever we feel pain, the usual response to protect ourselves from that state of vulnerability is anger.

Rejection is actually a normal stage in grief, but sometimes, unfortunately, it gains a foothold. It can be one of the causes for the deterioration and eventual breakup of a marriage. You must have tremendous emotional courage to admit and face all your feelings, even the ones you detest. But if you don't accept them, you may not fully accept yourself.

Perhaps there are days when you're accepting and others when you're put off or repulsed. Admit those feelings to yourself. Face them. Talk them over with another person, and especially go before the Lord with them. Talk with Him out loud, as though you were talking with a friend in the same room.

Don't hold back how you feel—no matter how unpleasant your feelings. No one is (or should be) judging you for them. You're probably harder on yourself than anyone else is. Some children are not pretty when they're born with certain conditions or when they're in intensive care, practically unrecognizable because of all the tubes sticking out of them. Accept your feelings of rejection as normal.

One of the most unsettling, yet common, feelings is anger. Whenever we feel pain, the usual response to protect ourselves from that state of vulnerability is anger. It's a normal reaction, but it can be the hardest of all the emotions to handle. It frightens us. We're afraid of the intensity of the feeling, of the possibility of losing control, and of what we might do.

In many cases of a child's disability, the actual cause is unknown. So even though the anger and protest are there, it's difficult to know what to be angry at. Lacking a clear direction for your anger is uncomfortable. Everything and everyone ends up becoming a potential target for this feeling of irritation. You have a vague sense of dissatisfaction with life and a floating sense of anxiety. These sentiments feed the anger, and the search for a suitable receptacle begins.

Often, the anger activates guilt feelings as well. Some parents wish their disabled child would just go ahead and die to alleviate family trials that they foresee for years and years to come. A child who rebels can be a source of embarrassment, and the parents wish the child would just disappear. Their anger may take the form of questions:

"Why me?"

"Why, God, why? It isn't fair!"

"What did we do to deserve this?"

"How will we be able to care for this child with so many needs?"

If you're in that situation, you may be frustrated by the lack of answers and the senselessness of it all. Your feelings fluctuate, as described by this parent of a disabled child:

> You may feel anger at the child but then reason it away, knowing that the child hasn't done anything to deserve the anger except exist, and even that wasn't the child's choice, it was yours. You may then reject the child as a target of anger because it seems illogical and is therefore unacceptable. In addition, you may feel very ill at ease with conscious rejection of your own child and will not allow yourself to experience feelings of anger toward the child. In some cases, however, you may become so overwhelmed by anger that the child becomes a scapegoat for all that is wrong in your life. Child abuse is much higher in families with disabled children; the additional stress of caring for this child, added to other stressors in life, becomes too much for parents to bear.[5]

Who else receives the brunt of the anger? Often, whoever gets in the way. We look for places to lay blame in order to direct attention away from ourselves. With a disabled child, the blame will be directed toward whoever was responsible for the care of the child. It could be a doctor, hospital, midwife, nurse, cabdriver who was too slow, or city management that failed to keep the street in good repair. I heard one father say, "I'm so mad at that doctor! He botched the delivery, ruined our son, and then kept him alive. Look at what we have to deal with for the rest of our lives!"

Spouses become angry with each other and once again blame. One says, "This disability must be in your line. We've never had any problem like this before." Or one accuses, "If only you hadn't insisted on taking her to that camp! It's your fault we don't have a whole child!" If this has happened to you, realize that, in time, your anger or your spouse's will probably subside. The anger is a way of coping with the hurt.

Many parents of disabled children divorce, however. The stress of caring for the child can quickly erode the marriage. In a new revision of the Holmes-Rahe Stress Test by Georgia-Witkin, one of the many new items identified as major life stressors—caring for a disabled child—had a stress rating of 97 out of a possible 100. The only stressor higher on the scale was the death of a spouse.[6]

A major article in the *Orange County Register* focused on this stress. The writer said,

> Somewhere among spoonfuls of medicine, trips to the doctor and hospital vigils, parents of disabled children often lose their marriage and their patience. . . .
>
> About 70 percent of U. S. couples with disabled children get divorced, therapists say. . . .
>
> "Having a disabled child is one of those crises that make you or break you," said Linda Scott, who coordinates a support group for parents of critically ill children at Children's Hospital of Orange County. "It's a 24-hour stressor."
>
> Many parents overcome that stressor with flair, creating close, happy families, said Sally Kanarek, director of Parenthelp USA.
>
> Parents who don't succeed tend to fall into harmful—and often unwitting—patterns, therapists and disability specialists say. They include:
>
> • Blaming each other for the child's disability.

- Excluding one parent from child care, or otherwise making him or her feel left out.
- Failing to talk regularly with one another.
- Calling the child names or saying you are sorry he or she was born.
- Passively endangering the child—often by failing to learn enough about his or her needs.
- Ignoring the child or the child's siblings.
- Leaving the child with a troubled or ill-prepared baby sitter.[7]

I've talked to a number of parents who blame themselves. Sometimes they may have contributed to the problem, but in many cases they did nothing wrong. Perhaps blaming anyone or anything gives us back a

*One reason many parents turn their anger
on themselves is that they're really
angry at God.*

sense of control that's lost when there's a life-changing problem. It gives us a reason for what went wrong, whether it's rational or not.

One reason many parents turn their anger on themselves is that they're really angry at God. But they believe they're not supposed to be angry with God, let alone express it to Him. Perhaps we all believe, to some degree, that since we're Christians, we attend church, and so on, we'll be immune from life's tragedies. If we've done our part, we figure, why isn't God doing His? This parental struggle is described well by Gerald Mann, a pastor who discovered his daughter was mentally retarded:

> I married my high school sweetheart when I was twenty, and she was eighteen. Eleven months later our first daughter was born. During those months I also became a believer and began studying for the ministry.
>
> Before we even knew Lois was pregnant, she had German measles—Rubella, or "three day measles" as it was known then.

We didn't even know enough to worry. During the seventh month of pregnancy, someone mentioned there could be potential damage to the fetus. I immediately phoned the doctor, a country general practitioner. When I sounded alarmed, he scolded me. "Now, Jerry," he chided, "If your child has only four toes, or four fingers, or one foot; will you love it any less?"

"Oh, if that's all we're talking about," I said, "why, heck no!" But that wasn't *all* we were talking about. Our daughter was thirteen months old before we got "real" enough to start trying to find out what was wrong.

First a pediatrician said she was just hyperactive and a little behind in learning to talk. Then a neurologist checked her out and watched her play around in the office for about ten minutes. He took me into his office and shut the door. "She's severely retarded, son. My advice is to put her in an institution somewhere, take that pretty little wife of yours home, and get her pregnant again. Maybe your second one will come out okay."

I was a rich kid, a football star attending college on scholarship, and a newly converted believer. This just couldn't be!

I had given my life to follow in Jesus' steps and forego the wealth, power, and prestige awaiting me in the family's business. And my child, my only child, had been assaulted in the warmth of her mother's womb by an insidious, mindless virus which would alter our lives forever.

I had read the New Testament. Jesus healed, and He promised that we could, too, if we believed. And I believed. I placed my hands on little Cindy many a night, praying for her healing. When nothing happened, I was certain the fault had to lie with me. It certainly didn't lie with the child. Nor could it lie with God, for He was good and loving and delivered His people.[8]

Irrational Thoughts

When you first learn of your loss and even beyond, your thoughts won't always make sense or be rational. Rosemarie Cook describes some of these irrational thoughts, along with rational, healthy thoughts you can use to counter the negative ones:

IRRATIONAL THOUGHTS	RATIONAL THOUGHTS
I (we) must have done something to deserve this.	No one did anything. This is something that just happened.
God saw that things were going too well for me (us), so he sent this.	God doesn't inflict harm on innocent children to punish adults.
The child's problems exist so God can perform a miracle and bring others to salvation.	Miracles are always possible, but we can't claim to know the mind of God.
If I (we) devote my life to this child, I will show others what a good and deserving person I am.	My worth in Christ doesn't depend on what I do. If I make mistakes, I'm still okay with God.
Having this child will not change anything in our family. We will have a totally normal life.	We will have to adapt and adjust. Things will be very different from what we expected them to be.
We can't let others know that we don't always feel okay.	It's okay to be human and to let others know that we are.
I (we) can't bear this burden.	I can't bear this alone, but with God, all things are possible.
It is always an uphill fight; everyone is against me (us).	Not everyone is an enemy. I will find people who can be of support in my life.
So and so is to blame for all of this.	Trying to find and place blame can take a lot of my time and energy and may impede my relationships with others.[9]

Perhaps it's *acceptance* that we work toward during the difficult times with a child. I didn't say "Like it" or "Not wish it had never happened." But even with those feelings, we must accept the reality of what occurred, take charge of this detour in life, and reroute ourselves to the main thoroughfare of life:

Recovery from loss is like having to get off the main highway every so many miles because the direct route is under reconstruction. The road signs reroute you through little towns you hadn't expected to visit and over bumpy roads you hadn't wanted to bounce around on. You are basically traveling in the appropriate direction. On the map, however, the course you are following has the look of shark's teeth instead of a straight line. Although you are gradually getting there, you sometimes doubt that you will ever meet up with the finished highway.[10]

There's a difference between adjusting to the situation and accepting it. You can adjust yourself to what has happened and begin to learn to live with it instead of fighting it. That's a good beginning. Accepting the situation could be an ongoing process. There will be recurring times of adjustment and new acceptance at the various stages of your child's life or when you're confronted by something new.

Remember one vital thing: You desperately need the support and comfort of other people during your loss.

In 1987, the U. S. Department of Health Services said that by 1990, there would be more than 800,000 self-help groups. That number has increased since then.

You may know intellectually that being with people is the best thing for you, but emotionally, you don't want that. It may help to talk about your feelings with a nonjudgmental, caring, listening friend. Try writing down everything you're feeling, and then express it. This is not a one-time experience. You'll need to do it again and again. Some people run, walk fast, talk softly, scream, draw, pound on a bed—many forms of expression are open to you. The feelings will last for some time.

Jan and Ed lost their seven-year-old son. They describe an experience that happened in the year following his death:

> The first Christmas after Mark died, a neighbor Jan knew only slightly telephoned. She must have realized how difficult Christmas would be for Jan and Ed after losing their elder son. "I don't know if I should call," she said, "but I was just thinking you won't be buying Mark any presents this year . . ." The neighbor suddenly stopped talking and started crying.

Jan responded, saying, "It must have taken a lot of courage to call and say that." Now weeping also, Jan explained, "I'm not crying because your words hurt me but because it's a gift that you are remembering Mark."[11]

Remember, the purpose of grieving your loss is to get beyond the numbness to face your loss and work on adapting to it. The overall purpose of grief is to bring you to the point of making necessary changes so you can live with the loss in a healthy way. It's a matter of beginning with the question "Why did this happen to me?" and eventually moving to "How can I learn through this experience? How can I now go on with my life?" When the *how* question replaces the *why* question, you have started to live with the reality of the loss. *Why* questions reflect a search for meaning in loss. *How* questions reflect your search for ways to adjust to the loss.[12] Your eventual goal is to be able to say,

> This loss I've experienced is a crucial upset in my life. In fact, it is the worst thing that will ever happen to me. But is it the end of my life? No. I can still have a rich and fulfilling life. Grief has been my companion and has taught me much. I can use it to grow into a stronger person than I was before my loss.[13]

Chuck Swindoll always writes so realistically and helpfully about life's difficulties and crises. The loss you've experienced is a crisis. Consider what he says:

> Crisis crushes. And in crushing, it often refines and purifies. You may be discouraged today because the crushing has not yet led to a surrender. I've stood beside too many of the dying, ministered to too many of the broken and bruised to believe that crushing is an end in itself. Unfortunately however it usually takes the brutal blows of affliction to soften and penetrate hard hearts. Even though such blows often seem unfair.

Remember Alexander Solzhenitsyn's admission:

It was only when I lay there on rotting prison straw that I sensed within myself the first stirring of good. Gradually, it was disclosed to me that the line separating good and evil passes, not through states, nor between classes, nor between political parties either, but right through all human hearts. So, bless you, prison, for having been in my life.

Those words provide a perfect illustration of the psalmist's instruction:

Before I was afflicted I went astray,
but now I obey your word.
It was good for me to be afflicted
so that I might learn your decrees.

(Psalm 119:67, 71 NIV)[14]

Remember that during your loss, God will step in to comfort you, and you will discover His grace in a new way.

Five

When Any Child Dies

As we now know so clearly, the death of a child is unlike any other loss. It's a horrendous shock, no matter how it happens.

One of the most difficult and disturbing issues to handle is the wrongness of a child's death. It just shouldn't happen. It doesn't make sense. It's death out of turn. The parent often feels, *Why should I survive when our child, who should survive, didn't?* Death violates the cycle that children grow up and replace the old.

Years ago, when infectious diseases ran wild, child death was common. That has now changed, however, and most deaths occur naturally and expectedly among the elderly. Our society is prepared for death with this group and so handles it relatively well. But the thought-to-be-infrequent occurrence of child death is more traumatic.

When you lose a child, you also lose what your child represented to you. You feel victimized in so many ways. You feel as though you've lost part of yourself, or even part of your physical body. Those features in the child that bore resemblance to you or your spouse hit the hardest.

You will miss the physical interaction as well—the sight, sound, smell, and touch of your child. If you were still in the hands-on, care-giving stage with your child, this absence will be terribly painful.

Your child embodied your connection to the future, too, and that no longer exists. If your child was old enough to respond to you, you've lost a very special love source. That love was based on need, dependence, admiration, and appreciation, but now it's gone. You've lost some of your own treasured qualities and talents as well, for you saw some of those that you value most in your child. Further, you've lost the expectations and dreams you had for your child as he or she grew older. The anticipated years, full of so many special events, were ripped away from you.

You may also see your child's death as a failure on your part. You feel anger and frustration because of being unable to exert some control over what happened to your child.[1]

Dr. Therese Rando graphically describes this feeling:

> With the death of your child you have failed in the basic function of parenthood: taking care of the children and the family. You are supposed to protect and provide for your child. You are supposed to keep her from all harm. She should be the one who grows up healthy to bury you.
>
> When you "fail" at this, when your child dies, you may feel that you have failed at your most basic function.
>
> The death of any child is a monumental assault on your sense of identity. Because you cannot carry out your role of preserving your child, you may experience an oppressive sense of failure, a loss of power and ability, and a deep sense of being violated. Disillusionment, emptiness, and insecurity may follow, all of which stem from a diminished sense of self. And this can lead to the guilt which is such a common feature in parental grief.[2]

Parental guilt can take many forms. Some parents experience survival guilt, the feeling that it's not right that they're still alive and their child isn't. There can also be illness-related guilt, where the parent thinks some personal deficiency caused the child's sickness and death. Some parents experience guilt over the belief that in some unknown way they either contributed to their child's death or failed to protect the child. And some experience moral guilt over the belief that the child's death was punishment for *their* violation of some moral or religious code.[3] As Dr. Rando explains,

> In those situations where the death results from genetic or unex-

plained medical factors, parents often take on additional burdens of grief. They try to explain why their child died prematurely and violated the laws of nature. Parents hold themselves responsible for not producing a healthy child that could survive longer, and often feel deficient and worthless as a result. Often, when answers about the cause of death are not forthcoming, parents tend to search all the way back to the earliest prenatal experiences in attempts to identify the reason for the medical condition: "Perhaps it was because I took the aspirin when I was pregnant that she developed the beginnings of the illness that took her life at 11."[4]

Because of all these losses, your grief over the death of a child will be more intense and last longer than grief over the loss of anyone else. The death of a child has been called the ultimate bereavement. You need to accept this and let others know about it as well.

You'll continually struggle with anger—anger at what happened, at anyone you feel could have prevented it, at the unfairness of what transpired, at the disruption of your life, and at God. The anger will come and go for years.

As a bereaved parent, you'll have to "grow up with the loss." Parents tend to mark their lives by the events involving and accomplishments of their children. The dates when those events would have occurred will still come around, even though your child won't be there to experience them. The sixth birthday; the first teen birthday; the times when your child would have received a driver's license, graduated, married, and had children; all will bring a resurgence of your grief when you least expect it.

A Double Dose

When your child dies because of a terminal disease, you get a double dose of grief. Before your child's death, you grieve over the fact that your child is going to die. Afterward, you grieve the actual death. Even though you know it's going to occur and you've known that for weeks, months, or years, it's still devastating. We used to hear about this situation mostly with parents whose children had cancer, but more and more we hear it about children dying of AIDS.

The trauma of coping with a terminally ill child redefines your entire life. Perhaps you've never experienced it yourself, but we're called to be compassionate and supportive of others. Knowing what other parents

The trauma of coping with a terminally ill child redefines your entire life.

face may speak to your heart. When a child is dying, it's as though the future is canceled for a time. The entire focus is on the present. Priorities change, and future plans and dreams are jeopardized. If the future is considered at all, it's with dread. Listen to the words of fathers and mothers who lost a child after a long illness:

A mother whose 17-year-old son died of bone cancer:

There was no future for us. We were afraid of what tomorrow and the next day might bring. We learned to savor every good moment, every good day. We didn't allow ourselves to even think beyond that day. The future was a frightening place for us.

A mother whose eight-year-old son died of leukemia:

You concentrate on the good days and live for those. You have to grasp them as they come. You have to take the bad days too, but you want to get them over quickly. When you have a good day, you want it to last forever. You never want to let it go.

A father whose four-year-old son died of leukemia:

We had to readjust our whole life when Sam became ill. All our future plans had to be shelved. I didn't even want to think about the future because I knew it held Sam's death. It was just too unbearable to think about.

A mother whose six-year-old daughter died of leukemia:

Her death was not imminent to me. This was something in the future; it was far away. I lived only for today. I didn't even think about tomorrow, let alone plan for it.[5]

When your child is diagnosed as terminal, it may take days for reality to sink in. Listen to the response of these two parents:

I think nature prepares you for these times. You can only absorb a small amount of information at one time. You hear the words but they don't sink in. The true reality comes to you over a span of time—a little at a time. I know it was several hours before I was able to grasp the full weight of what was said to me and several days for the emotional impact to ripple through me.

A mother said:

We took Mark to a specialist who put him in the hospital for surgery the next day. We were confident of the outcome. I think I developed an optimism which supported me at that time. I went to the hospital alone with Mark and was waiting in the reception area when they called me into the hall. The doctor was standing there with his hands in his surgical gloves raised in front of him just like you see on TV. He had come out of surgery halfway through to talk with me. All he said was "I've got some bad news—it's cancer!" I just stood there. I don't think I ever in my life experienced that kind of feeling of shock! No preparation! Everything stopped! It was as if I was stuck to the floor! I couldn't move! I couldn't speak! I knew that hospital well but I couldn't even think what floor Mark's room was on. I walked up and down the corridors aimlessly. Those ugly words—"it's cancer"—were repeated over and over in my mind. I tried to call home but I couldn't even remember my own phone number![6]

If you were the parent of a terminally ill child, you probably experienced one or more of the following common reactions. You may not have accepted the diagnosis and prognosis when they were initially revealed to you. (This also happens when you're told your child has a disability.) You assimilate them gradually or deny them right up to the last moments with your child.

Perhaps you fantasized consciously or subconsciously about a miraculous recovery for your child.

You may have tried to bring about a healing yourself through arranging for a healing service, having the elders of the church anoint your child with oil and pray, providing a special diet, going for a special treatment banned in this country, using visualization techniques, or bargaining with God.

You may have felt your child's illness was some sort of punishment for something you did in the past or even thought about.[7]

Impact on Marriage

No matter how you lost a child, the questions arise: "How do I recover? What steps can I take to survive?" We've looked at loss and grief in an overall manner, but let's consider other aspects now.

Following the death of a child, a marriage tends to flounder. It's as though the very structure of your family life is under attack. You may have to intervene with your other children as they react to the loss of their brother or sister. You and your spouse may struggle with vocational pressures because of being distracted and absent from your job for an extended period. Daily routines seem overwhelming because of your grief, and you may pick at each other when you see things left undone. There could be a new financial burden because of the child's illness or the unbelievably high expense of a funeral. All these elements add to the marital tension.

It's estimated that 90 percent of all couples who lose a child face some kind of marital struggles within the first year after the death. The divorce rate is high among couples who have lost an only child.[8] Statistics also show that in approximately 70 percent of the families where a child was killed violently, parents either separated or divorced.[9] Many marriages that dissolve were held together by a slim thread to begin with, and this event seemed to shatter the remaining strands. It could also be that the parenting roles were more intense than the marital relationship.

The death of a child, however, does not have to lead to divorce. It can become a time of mutual comfort, support, and growth.

Shadow Grief

No parent is ever prepared to lose a child, regardless of the cause or the child's age. But you can *learn* to recover and survive, and it is a learning process. There are no shortcuts to your grieving. It's painful and long, and you will wish it would go away. You're living in a dark tunnel, and you're not sure there's any light at the end. But when you keep searching for it, you will find it. This grief lingers longer than any other, and you carry the remnants of shadow grief for years.

Most of us don't realize there's a pattern of peaks and valleys in grief.

Ronald Knapp gives us an insightful description of shadow grief:

Shadow grief reveals itself more in the form of an emotional "dullness," where the person is unable to respond fully and completely to outer stimulation and where normal activity is moderately inhibited. It is characterized as a dull ache in the background of one's feelings that remains fairly constant and that, under certain circumstances and on certain occasions, comes bubbling to the surface, sometimes in the form of tears, sometimes not, but always accompanied by a feeling of sadness and a mild sense of anxiety. Shadow grief will vary in intensity depending on the person and the unique factors involved. It is more emotional for some than for others.

Where shadow grief exists, the individual can never remember the events surrounding the loss without feeling some kind of emotional reaction, regardless of how mild.

The difference between "normal" grief and "shadow" grief is

similar to the difference between pneumonia and the common cold. The latter is less serious, less disruptive to life, more of a nuisance than anything else.[10]

No one can tell you how long this grief will last. Grief has a beginning, a middle, and an end. But many parents get stuck in the middle, and most don't understand the dynamics and duration of grief, which makes it even more difficult to adjust.

Most of us don't realize there's a pattern of peaks and valleys in grief. Look at the intensity of grief as indicated by this chart:

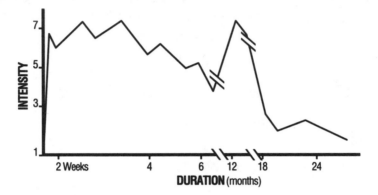

Notice the jagged peaks. The pain and grief actually intensify at three months and then gradually subside, but not steadily. They go up and down. Most people don't need a reminder of the first-year anniversary of the loss of a loved one. The grief comes rushing in with pain that rivals the initial feelings. If anyone tries to tell you that you should be "over it by now" or "feeling better" at any of those peak times, you may become quite upset. That's understandable. It's also understandable that people don't appreciate the grief process unless they've been through it themselves.[11]

You may want to give this section of the book or the chart to those around you to help them understand. Or ask your minister to explain these facts to your congregation.

The usual time for recovering from the loss of a loved one is two years, but throw away that measure when dealing with the loss of a child; it will be longer.

The Healing Power of Tears

Your tears will come for years. Let them. One morning they hit me in our worship service at Hollywood Presbyterian Church. The service focused on Pentecost. As the organ played, the sound of a brass quartet suddenly filled the air. Trumpets always brought a response from Matthew. He would look up with an alertness or wonderment in his expression, as if to say, "Oh, that's something new."

The sound of the brass in the service brought back another memory: Matthew's joyful laughter. Several years ago, I decided to take up the trumpet (which lasted only a few years). I purchased a horn and took weekly lessons. During one of Matthew's visits home, I began to practice. He looked at me with an expression that said, "I don't believe what I'm hearing!" He listened to another squawk, threw back his head, and laughed harder than we had ever heard him laugh. Again and again, he laughed and giggled until we were all in stitches. My novice attempts to play had at least pleased him. Needless to say, these memories brought the tears once again.

Another time, I was driving home and listening to Chuck Swindoll's radio program. During the message, he listed the names of the disciples. Hearing him say the name *Matthew* brought my sense of loss and sadness to the surface, where it stayed for several days. Who would have thought that would have happened?

Then there are times when my feelings are just flat. A low-grade numbness sets in, and I wonder when the pain will hit again. Just three months after Matthew died, I had been very busy with work and projects. For several days, there had been little feeling and no tears. As I told a client what had happened, however, the tears came to my eyes. Then as I sat with the parents of a profoundly disabled child, trying to help them, the tears again rose to the surface. Next I received a note from a friend who had lost his 19-year-old son in an accident more than four years earlier. When he said the pain was sometimes still as fresh as if it had just happened, I wondered, *Will it be that way for us?* Again my eyes clouded over.

During that dry time, as I refer to it, grief hit hard once more. I was riding my exercise bike and listening to a worship tape by Terry Clark.

One of the songs was "I Remember." As I rode, I was also working on a new catalog to send to people who had attended our seminars over the years. I was wondering whether to include anything about Matthew, since most of the people had heard our story. I had considered saying, "For years we had prayed for Matthew to be whole. On March 15, God saw fit to make him whole."

As I thought about that (and perhaps because of the music and the fact that I was planning to visit his grave for the first time), the flood occurred. The sense of loss was overwhelming, and I wept intensely. One thing I've learned—you never need to apologize for your tears.[12]

Just in writing this chapter and looking once again at some of the notes we received and my written thoughts, the feelings and tears rose once more to the surface. I found two written responses to my tears that I had put in a folder. This first one I wrote nine months after Matthew's death:

January 5, 1991

Where have the tears gone? There was a time when I thought they would never end, but now I miss them as though they were a friend. There's only a mist where once a stream, the memories are fading all too fast, like it was last night's dream. It seems too soon to be this way, but I realize they may return yet another day. Who would have thought the sobs and clouded eyes would be missed, but they are. And yet, even as this is written, the words are difficult to see for some strange reason.

The poems and letters from friends help to bring back the loss again. Words of comfort expressed at the time of deepest pain help to keep Matthew's memory alive. For that's all we have of him now are memories. Someone else has the joy of his presence, his laugh, his smile, and his hugs.

Where have they gone? They haven't. They were hiding and waiting once again for the time to be called out and express the loss. They're here again, not as an intruder, but as a welcomed friend. Please don't stay away so long the next time. I need you. We need you.

Then in the fifteenth month, I wrote,

> It's been some time since the feelings came to the surface. You
> begin to wonder if they ever will again. But then they do. And
> each time is different. It began with finding some old pictures of
> Matthew when he was quite young and in most of them he was
> smiling. Two days later we were watching Dr. Ogilvie on a Sunday
> morning TV program, and he read the passage in which the cen-
> turion came to Jesus about his son who was dying. Jesus told him
> to go home, his son would live. Both Joyce and I had the same
> response: "I wish that Jesus would have made that statement to
> us about Matthew." The tears came that morning. They will
> always be there and come when you least expect them. But they
> are there as part of our connection with something that we val-
> ued but lost, at least for the present time. They are also a
> reminder that our life is a series of transitions and changes, some
> of which we like and others we resist.

You can recover. It will take an understanding of the grief process, a
change of attitude from thinking *It will never end* to *I will adjust and survive,* and a willingness to make the painful journey through the wilder-
ness of grief.

Most parents want to discover how to cope with their loss. Coping is
tied to mourning, though. *Coping* means "struggling or contending with
some success." An older meaning was to "strike back or fight." Mourning
is all about actively and willingly working through your grief, striking or
fighting back. It's the process of purging yourself of the grief over your
loss.[13]

Ann Kaiser Stearns says, "All of us feel powerless at times because we
are human beings. Triumphant survivors, however, trade in the position
of helplessness for a decision to take charge and search for options."[14]

A unique factor is involved in the loss of a child. It's perhaps best
summarized by the phrase "to never forget." Ronald Knapp describes it:

> One important commonality that appeared to be characteristic
> of all parents who have suffered the loss of a child for whatever

reason took the form of a need or desire: a need that makes the loss of a child different from other kinds of losses, and one that truly complicates the normal process of grieving. This is the need or desire never to forget—or to remember always!

The child is gone! Out of sight! And parents, mothers particularly, harbor a great fear that what memories they have of the child may eventually fade away. They fear that they will forget the sight of the child's face, the sound of his or her voice, the texture of the child's hair, the uniqueness of the hands, even the child's characteristic smell. Parents severely miss these sensual experiences and eventually come to wish to retain them in memory for as long as they live.[15]

Helpful Steps

As you grieve, keep in mind certain steps that may be helpful. We've already talked about guilt, but a major task is to break the guilt connection. The longer you let it linger, the more it gains a foothold and takes up permanent residence. Self-blame will cripple you and your other family relationships. It may be guilt over something you did, didn't do, thought, or wished.

If others around you don't talk about the death or seem to avoid you or the subject, you may feel even more guilty, as though you did something wrong. But people avoid the subject for reasons that have nothing to do with blaming you. Most don't know what to say, and many feel anxiety over your child's death. They feel threatened. As a bereaved parent, you repre-

In a loving, gentle way, you need to let others know you will not be ignored.

sent their worst fears; if it happened to your child, it could happen to theirs.

Unfortunately, such a calloused response leaves you without support and fails to provide the validation you need about what has happened. Nothing hurts more than being ignored.[16]

You may have to take the initiative to break the silence. When you talk about your child and what you experienced, you let others know it's acceptable to discuss the death. If you feel you're being avoided, go to others and start conversations. Use a letter to help people know what you've experienced and how they can respond to you (as described in chapter 10). That makes it easier to bring up the subject.

In a loving, gentle way, you need to let others know you will not be ignored. Then you will receive more care and support. Many are concerned that talking about your loss will intensify your pain. In some of the caring cards we received, we read statements like, "I hope this letter or card hasn't increased your hurt." But even if it did bring our pain to the surface, the comfort from the card was worth it all. Two of the caring notes came from one of Matthew's home staff and one of his teachers:

Dear Mr. and Mrs. Wright,

It was a joy working with Matthew. He had such an infectious laugh! He would look at you from the corner of his eye, half-smiling as if to say, "I'm going to make my move when you're not watching me"—which is just what he did! He was becoming more sure of himself, more independent. He had learned to trust me, to let me prompt and encourage him without pulling away as much. This means a great deal to me.

I'll always remember the way Matthew moaned when enjoying a good meal, and the way he loved to splash when taking a bath . . .

Dear Mr. and Mrs. Wright,

This letter is late coming I know, but it has been very difficult for me to sit down and actually acknowledge the sad fact that Matthew was taken from us. I felt many other ones would be taken before Matthew.

It was just at Christmas time I was remembering taking Matthew and Debra to the mall at Christmas time the year before. He kept trying to sneak off on me, and I would get so tickled at him and the expression he would give me when he saw me behind him. They both, and me too, enjoyed that day so much. Matthew was one that I have missed the most since leaving Dominga School.

I know there is not much I can say, but please realize that Matthew gave so much pleasure to so many and he was a joy for Dominga to have. He was always so neat and clean and full of surprises for us. His absence from school was always a disappointment for us . . .

What are your sources of support? Find them. Identify them. Don't withdraw, even if you feel like doing so, as you will. Find a supportive person(s) and a group. The person needs to be accessible and available, experienced with a loss similar to yours, able to help you go on with your life, and able to help with tasks and errands you're unable to do during the grieving period.[17] (For support groups, see the appendix at the end of this book.)

You can expect something else to occur if and when you struggle with guilt, too: You're likely to concentrate on how perfect or good your child was. You tend to exalt all your child's positive traits, to idealize him or her. You think of your child as the "best," the "most loving," or the "most special."

If that happens, you're overfocusing on the one who was lost and paying increased attention to what you're missing and longing for. If you have other children, you may be comparing them unfavorably. They make mistakes and drive you up the wall. Deceased children don't do that. They're saints, frozen in time. This is somewhat normal for a while, but in time, you'll be able to recall both the positive and the negative experiences, and a balance will return.[18]

As you work through recovery, you may discover you have developed a new attitude toward death and your own dying. Studies show that parents tend to no longer view death as their enemy. Many find that it could be a friend, especially those whose child went through a painful, lingering illness. For them, death became a release and a relief. And as they dealt with their child's death, they were able to handle the deaths of others more effectively. Isn't it interesting that it often takes this experience to make the truth of God's Word become a reality?

Three Suggestions

As you proceed through your valley of recovery, try these three suggestions that have meant the most to me. First, *pray*. Write out your prayers as you may write out your feelings at times. Don't edit your prayers; let your feelings flow. Second, *worship*—at home and in church, as though you're the only person there. Don't worry about what others might think of your feelings and tears. Third, *read Scripture*. Let the comfort of God's Word meet your needs. Read comforting passages again and again, to yourself and aloud.

God's words, spoken to us in time of need, give us the ability to survive. Here is a brief collection of promises for those who mourn:

> In all their distress he too was distressed,
> and the angel of his presence saved them.
> In his love and mercy he redeemed them;
> he lifted them up and carried them
> all the days of old. (Isa. 63:9)

> The LORD is my shepherd. (Ps. 23:1*a*)

> For God so loved the world that he gave his one and only Son, that whoever believes in him shall not perish but have eternal life. (John 3:16)

> I am the resurrection and the life. He who believes in me will live, even though he dies; and whoever lives and believes in me will never die. (John 11:25-26)

> God will wipe away every tear from their eyes. (Rev. 7:17*b*)

> He who goes out weeping, carrying seed to sow, will return with songs of joy, carrying sheaves with him. (Ps. 126:6)

Blessed are those who mourn, for they will be comforted. (Matt. 5:4)

Come to me, all you who are weary and burdened, and I will give you rest. (Matt. 11:28)

Praise be to the God and Father of our Lord Jesus Christ, the Father of compassion and the God of all comfort, who comforts us in all our troubles. (2 Cor. 1:3-4*a*)

When you pass through the waters, I will be with you; and when you pass through the rivers, they will not sweep over you. When you walk through the fire, you will not be burned; the flames will not set you ablaze. (Isa. 43:2)

The Spirit helps us in our weakness. We do not know what we ought to pray, but the Spirit himself intercedes for us with groans that words cannot express. (Rom. 8:26)

For I am convinced that neither death nor life, neither angels nor demons, neither the present nor the future, nor any powers, neither height nor depth, nor anything else in all creation, will be able to separate us from the love of God that is in Christ Jesus our Lord. (Rom. 8:38-39)

My grace is sufficient for you, for my power is made perfect in weakness. (2 Cor. 12:9)

Ask all the questions you need to ask, again and again.

Often parents and others ask, "Where do children go when they die?" I believe the Scriptures tell us they go to heaven, into the presence of God. David had an infant son who died when he was only seven days old. David's response indicates he believed his son was somewhere to which he, too, would go one day. And that somewhere is *heaven*.

When anyone dies, the soul leaves the body. Our bodies are simply "tents." Paul said that when we're away from the body, we're at home with the Lord (see 2 Cor. 5:8). He also seemed to indicate that when Christians die, they awake in glory (see 1 Thess. 4:14).

Be patient with your recovery, but believe you will recover. David Wiersbe offers good advice about believing:

> In grief God seems to have abandoned us. He hasn't. In grief we feel as if nothing matters. It does. Sometimes we think life is not worth living; it is! In times of sorrow people of faith have to "believe against the grain." In our weakness, God reveals his strength, and we do more than we thought possible.
>
> Faith means clinging to God in spite of circumstances. It means following him when we cannot see, being faithful to him when we don't feel like it.
>
> Mourners need a creed; it is "I believe!" We need to affirm this creed daily:
>
> • I believe God's promises are true.
> • I believe heaven is real.
> • I believe I will see my child again.
> • I believe God will see me through.
> • I believe nothing can separate me from God's love.
> • I believe God has work for me to do.
>
> "Believing against the grain" means having a survivalist attitude. Bereaved parents are survivors; they have endured. Not only do they survive, but also out of grief they create something good.[19]

In time, as other parents have, you will find meaning in what you've experienced. Listen to the words of these parents:

> I really don't know why this happened to us, but I've stopped looking for the answer! I just have to put my faith in the Lord's hands. . . . Only He knows—only He has the answers!

> The Lord works in many strange ways. At first I simply could not fathom this, but then I accepted the Lord. . . . He must have had

His reasons, and these—whatever they are—are good enough for me.

At first I was confused and bewildered and angry. Why did this happen to us? Why did God permit this to happen? . . . Then I began to realize that it was the will of God. . . . Who am I to question further?

Nothing pacified me after Tommy's death. I couldn't understand how a loving God could allow such a thing. . . . However, I eventually came to realize that God was my greatest salvation; whatever His reasons are for taking Tommy, I can now accept them! I think of Him as holding Tommy in His arms until the day I can join him.

"The Lord giveth and the Lord taketh away"—that is a quote from the Bible! I never knew exactly what it meant until this thing happened. . . . You're right, I questioned! I was angry and filled with hate over the loss of our son. . . . However, the anger and hate softened as I accepted the Lord. I put myself in His hands and immediately felt a sense of peace overtake me.[20]

Saying Good-Bye

In an earlier chapter, we talked about saying good-bye to Matthew. We have said it many times now in various ways. Visiting the gravesite is one. Redecorating a child's room or finally giving away his clothes is another. I've read the good-bye letters that some have written to a loved one who has died. But when a young child dies, I believe there's a difference.

When a Christian or a young child dies, those who are left behind have to say good-bye. But the one who died is able to say hello to the Lord. This is why our feelings can sometimes be a mixture—we are saddened by our loss, but there's also a sense of joy for what the deceased person is now experiencing. We've felt this. We have a void in our lives, but Matthew's life is now full and complete. The Christian death is a transition, a tunnel leading from this world into the next. This transition can be depicted in many ways.

A month after Matthew died, I received a copy of Max Lucado's inspirational book *The Applause of Heaven.* I had heard about the book, especially the final chapter. So I did what I normally don't: I went immedi-

> *The Christian death is a transition, a tunnel leading from this world into the next.*

ately to the final chapter and read it first. He begins by describing his conclusion to a long trip and finally arriving at the airport. His wife and three daughters are excited that he's home. But one of them has an interesting response. In the midst of the shouts of joy, she stops long enough to clap. She applauds him. Isn't that different? But it's also affirming and appropriate.

Then Lucado talks about the Christian's ultimate home and home-going and what might happen there. He begins by quoting Revelation 21:1-5:

> "Then I saw a new heaven and a new earth, for the first heaven and the first earth had passed away, and there was no longer any sea. I saw the Holy City, the new Jerusalem, coming down out of heaven from God, prepared as a bride beautifully dressed for her husband. And I heard a loud voice from the throne saying, 'Now the dwelling of God is with men, and he will live with them. They will be his people, and God himself will be with them and be their God. He will wipe every tear from their eyes. There will be no more death or mourning or crying or pain, for the old order of things has passed away.'"

John says that someday God will wipe away your tears. The same hands that stretched the heavens will touch your cheeks. The same hands that formed the mountains will caress your face. The same hands that curled in agony as the Roman spike cut through will someday cup your face and brush away your tears forever.

When you think of a world where there will be no reason to cry, ever, doesn't it make you want to go home?

"There will be no more death . . ." John declares. Can you imagine it? A world with no hearses or morgues or cemeteries or tombstones? Can you imagine a world with no spades of dirt thrown on caskets? No names chiseled into marble? No funerals? No black dresses? No black wreaths?

In the next world, John says, "good-bye" will never be spoken.[21]

Every person on earth is appointed to die at some time. We fear it, resist it, try to postpone it, and even deny its existence. But it won't work. We can't keep our loved ones from dying. We can't keep ourselves from dying. But we can see death from God's perspective. Lucado concludes his book with what homegoing means from a new point of view:

> Before you know it, your appointed arrival time will come; you'll descend the ramp and enter the City. You'll see faces that are waiting for you. You'll hear your name spoken by those you love. And, maybe, just maybe—in the back, behind the crowds—the One who would rather die than live without you will remove his pierced hands from his heavenly robe and. . . applaud.[22]

I just sat there quietly after reading that, letting it minister to me. I could see Jesus responding that way as Matthew arrived. It's true—our loved ones who died are saying hello. We have said good-bye to them. It's true—we say hello to each new day without them, but only for now!

⧼Six⧽

Special Losses

LOSING a child is always difficult—for all the reasons we've discussed. But parents who lose a very young child often face an even harder time, for stillbirths and the death of an infant are usually not considered as serious as the loss of an older child. There seems to be an attitude that says, "In a child's death, the younger the child, the easier it is; the older the child, the harder it is." In the past, society viewed survivors of miscarriages as illegitimate mourners.

But today, circumstances are much different. Families are changing. Choosing to have only one or two children, having children at an older age, and the struggles of raising children as a single parent all make for smaller families. We also seem to have more and more couples who are unable to have children of their own. This is a major loss that frequently isn't recognized, so encouragement and support from others are often lacking. We want to address these other losses in this chapter.

A Common Pain

When a miscarriage occurs, as it does in as many as 25 percent of all pregnancies, the couple often receive little or no support. And whatever comfort is offered doesn't last long. In many cases, the expectant mother wasn't even showing, so no one but her spouse assists in the bereavement or shares in the memories.

The intensity and amount of grief are tied not to the length of time the unborn child was carried but to the hopes, values, needs, feelings, and expectations the parents had placed on that child. Parents begin to bond with the child before birth. They celebrate the news of pregnancy and usually share it quickly. They dream of the baby's first step or a family Christmas and often run through the child's life in their own minds.

When the miscarriage occurs, the dreams die as well. And can you imagine the intensity of the grief when a couple has been trying for a child for years or the husband and wife are approaching age 40? The grief can also be intensified if there's a continual string of miscarriages. Multiple miscarriages are a real possibility for many couples. In one study of 1,010 family members who had experienced a miscarriage, the mothers averaged 1.9 miscarriages. One mother said she had experienced 15 miscarriages; only one child out of 16 pregnancies survived. Her marriage didn't make it.[1] Studies indicate that with a miscarriage, the "average recovery time" is approximately nine to 15 months.[2]

Following a miscarriage, too often the statements of others do little to relieve the grief. People say, "You're young; you can try again." "You're probably better off. Something could have been wrong with the child anyway, and that would have been so hard." "Well, in a sense it's good it happened to you since you're a strong person and can handle it. I never could."

If you've suffered a miscarriage, let your grief be known. If it has happened to acquaintances, reach out and help them grieve.

You're free to grieve as much as you feel the need to.

Sometimes parents want to see the miscarried child, and sometimes they don't. Some parents are given Polaroid pictures of the ultrasound tracing of the child if he or she was old enough. That helps to make the situation more real. Some name their child and have a service for him or her.

One couple I worked with knew at four months that their child had a rare condition and would not go full term. At six months the little girl died, and the father told me how he took her outside and held her as he looked at the stars, prayed over her, and committed her to the Lord.

If other people don't understand what you're doing and try to give you counteradvice, just remember that they usually are not experts and are speaking out of their own anxiety and dismay. You're free to grieve as much as you feel the need to. Be aware that the anniversary of when the child was to be born will hit you, and that it could continue to do so for years.[3]

Abortion is another major form of loss today. Whether it was therapeutic or elective, it still involves the loss of a child, and it needs to be grieved. In our society, women are not encouraged to grieve over an abortion; they're supposed to be pleased and relieved rather than sad. But that's not realistic.

> Vicky Thorn of *Project Rachel* reports that women generally have not been helped by easy dismissal of guilt. "When women are told, 'Don't worry about it. You did the best you could under the circumstances. Get on with your life,' it hasn't proven helpful for them. They inwardly feel the abortion was wrong, and they want and need someone to be honest with them and say, 'Yes, it is wrong to take a baby's life.' They can then accept that fact and get on with mourning."[4]

The grief response for women who have abortions is often different from that for other types of loss. Some feel relief and happiness that it's over. But many repress and deny their real feelings of loss and guilt for a prolonged period. They may not surface for years. I have seen this occur time and again in the counseling office. It's not just women who experience this loss, either; men do as well.

If you experienced abortion or know someone who has, reach out and take the steps necessary for you or the other person to discover forgiveness and recovery through the grief process.

Stillbirth is a frequent form of loss, although the tendency is to believe it happens to other families. One out of every hundred births is a stillbirth. When it occurs, it's more devastating than a miscarriage because the parents feel they have passed through the risky period, and everything should be all right. There has also been more time for bonding. Everyone has been getting ready for the birth and the baby shower. Announcements have been purchased, prospective baby-sitters selected.

But when the baby is born, there is no cry, no breath, no life. The parents are shocked.

Once again, other people will find it hard to help with the loss, because the baby didn't exist for them. The mom and dad feel isolated, and when they're admonished to go on with life and plan for another child, they get no encouragement to grieve. But they have a need and a right to grieve and to take whatever steps are necessary. I've talked with couples whose experience was all too common. Family members strongly suggested that autopsies and funeral services be forgotten to make the loss easier for them. But that approach actually makes it more difficult.

After a miscarriage or stillbirth, parents question themselves and each other. The pregnancy and birth are analyzed again and again in the following ways:

Reviewing the pregnancy:

- What happened during my pregnancy that didn't happen to people with healthy babies? What did I do wrong?
- How many hours did I sleep each night? Did I sleep too much or too little? Should I have taken a nap in the afternoon?
- How many cigarettes did I have a day?
- How many cocktails did I have during my pregnancy?
- Did I run down the stairs or did I merely walk fast?
- Did I try to exercise too much? Didn't I get enough exercise?
- Should I have abstained from sexual intercourse?
- Did I think something that made the baby die?

Reviewing the birth:

- Did I select the wrong doctor?
- Did I go to the hospital too late in labor?
- Should I have refused an anesthetic?
- Should I not have attempted a natural childbirth?
- Didn't I try hard enough?

The questions are varied and many, depending on your individual circumstances. As you continue to review the pregnancy and birth, you define the boundaries of what you perceive as having been your personal responsibility. You release some of the guilt and begin the long, slow process of fully acknowledging your loss. As long as guilt is the major issue, the baby cannot be relinquished. The baby is held onto with "If only's." If only I hadn't run . . . or stayed up the night before . . . or eaten too much . . . or cried too much . . . or taken a diuretic . . . and on and on.

Along with the guilt you inflict on yourself, is the guilt you either assume or imagine coming from other people. For example, some husbands intentionally or inadvertently insinuate the child's life was in the wife's domain, thereby implying she should have prevented the death. Even the idle remarks of relatives or friends can reinforce existing guilt or produce new guilts. The father who says, "I told you to quit smoking!"; the sister who self-righteously proclaims, "My doctor told me not to drink at all during pregnancy, and I didn't"; the neighbor who asks, "Weren't you still going to work in your eighth month?" adds to your self-blame.[5]

Parents who suffer a stillbirth need to validate and confirm the child's existence by seeing, holding, touching, naming, praying over, and burying their baby. When they don't, they are left with doubts that they actually had the child. I heard of one woman who went to the market and weighed vegetables to find one the weight and height of her stillborn child that she had not been allowed to see or hold, leaving her without a memory.

Parents need to take steps to make the baby real to them. One such step is, as a couple, to review your thoughts and feelings about—and experiences with—the baby throughout the length of the pregnancy. It's also most helpful, whether the problem is an inability to conceive, a miscarriage, or a stillbirth, to find a support group with others who have just gone through the same experience.[6]

Precious Little Ones

Newborn children die, too, and that's different from a stillbirth loss because the parents have had some time to know and bond with a living child. Their grief is similar to that of losing an older child. But some factors still hinder grief recovery. Others may downplay the child's death, and when a loss is discounted, grief work is hampered.

Why may others seem insensitive? Most people don't know anyone who has lost a newborn, so they don't know how to respond. They didn't know your baby and thus can't really join you emotionally in your grief. Even hospitals engage in "protective" behavior that hampers a mother's grief by moving her from the obstetric ward to another location so she will not be reminded of her experience.

Statements like these are never helpful: "You're fortunate you didn't have time to get really attached." "You can be glad you hadn't taken him home yet." They negate the fact of a parent's love and the bonding that already occurred. Sometimes before the mother has a chance to leave the hospital, friends and relatives go into her home and remove all indications that she would have had a baby there. But the desire to shield her from the pain won't help her grieve.

One of the most stressful types of newborn death is sudden infant death syndrome (SIDS). It's the sudden and unexpected death of what appeared to be a healthy infant. The death remains unexplained, even after a thorough postmortem exam. This is a real medical dilemma. It's the largest cause of death among infants between the ages of two weeks and one year, with the greatest number of deaths occurring between two and four months.[7]

This problem is at least as old as Old Testament times and seems to have occurred as frequently in the eighteenth and nineteenth centuries as it does now. Is it possible to predict? No. Can it be prevented by a physician? No. It's not caused by suffocation, neglect, aspiration or regurgitation, pneumonia, heart attack, or by changing modes of infant care. It isn't hereditary or contagious. It does appear to be more common, however, among the lower socioeconomic classes.

Many theories exist about the cause, but no answers.[8] Because SIDS strikes with the suddenness of an earthquake and without warning, these deaths devastate the remaining family members, generating an abundance of guilt and anger.

There's an overwhelming sense of shock and disbelief when a healthy infant is found dead. Then comes an unrestrained welling up of a "No!" that cannot be shouted loud enough. This death seems impossible, for the last few hours before the baby was put to bed were normal. The baby didn't cry or otherwise indicate a problem. The baby went to bed so many times before and always woke up later. But this time, it didn't happen.

The result is self-imposed guilt, blame, and hate. "What did I do or not do that caused this? Where did I go wrong?" If the baby died in the care of someone else, such as a baby-sitter or relative, that person may have to face accusations about doing or failing to do something significant.

Because of the nature of SIDS, police, medical examiners, or hospital personnel may investigate the death. Sometimes the parents, in the midst of their grief and guilt, have to deal with accusations from those investigators. And even when the official interrogation is concluded, parents continue to grill themselves, looking for a cause and a reason. As one parent said,

> You rehearse everything you did prior to the baby's death. You consider the clothing of the baby, the way the crib was prepared, the temperature of the room, what the baby ate or didn't eat. Was there a sigh, a cough, a cry, an irritability or dullness that escaped your notice? You may recall a gesture or a sound that, upon reflection, you decide was a signal of your baby's distress when, in fact, it is only a product of your desperate imagination.[9]

Parents who lose a child to SIDS are terribly vulnerable emotionally. There is no letup, and they usually have to explain the death of their baby over and over. "What did the baby die of? Weren't you home? How often did you check her? Did the baby choke? smother?"—all the repetitive questions increase guilt and anxiety. Delores Kuenning identifies yet another problem:

> Friends and family are often afraid to talk to parents—because

they don't know what to say, they don't say anything. This adds to the SIDS parents' isolation.

One mother said, "You feel so isolated within yourself. When people withdraw from you because of their own discomfort, in a way, it's almost like an accusation that you were at fault. You feel you must have done something wrong, or this wouldn't be happening to you. On the other hand, you almost feel like they don't want to be around you because they feel it might be catching. I know people don't know what to say. I would rather they'd come and be with me or ask permission, 'Would you like someone to be with you?' rather than feel, 'Well, I don't know what to say so I think I'll stay away.'"

Another added, "Friends who have well babies often don't know what to do about visiting. Sometimes it is just too painful for the parent to see another baby right at that moment. Some SIDS parents find this painful for as long as a year. I suggest the friend call and simply ask how the parents feel about seeing other babies."

The first mother *wanted* to see other children. "I wanted to see there were children out there who were living and laughing and okay. I needed to see and feel and hope that I could again have that someday. It is always better to ask how the parent feels than to assume they do or do not want to see other babies."[10]

When sudden death occurs, a parent may deny the baby died. A mother continues doing what she did before—functioning as the baby's parent. She may continue to clean and arrange the nursery, prepare formula, or fix the baby's clothes. It's a denial to protect against the crushing ache of the loss. When the shock subsides, withdrawal from outsiders and even the family is common. Dreams may contain the theme of searching for, caring for, and playing with the baby.

Recovering from Your Loss

In any loss, you have to recognize and accept the fact and the feelings. You'll live in the valley of loss for a portion of your life. Don't fight it. You can't. Face it and take charge of it. It's a step in recovery. C. S. Lewis, the author of *Mere Christianity* and *The Screwtape Letters*, didn't marry until later in life, and after just four years of marriage, his wife, Joy, died of cancer. In his book *A Grief Observed*, he said,

> I once read the sentence, "I lay awake all night with a toothache, thinking about the toothache and about lying awake." That's true to life. Part of every misery is, so to speak, the misery's shadow or reflection: the fact that you don't merely suffer but have to keep on thinking about the fact that you suffer. I not only live each endless day in grief, but live each day thinking about living each day in grief.[11]

It's true that the awareness of how much you hurt can cause even greater hurt, but the realization that the hurt is not permanent can lessen it. It won't last forever, but it will come in waves, and you'll feel one come crashing in unexpectedly from time to time. It's just like ocean waves hitting the shore. Afterward, there's a time of calm.

God does not allow us to experience more than we can handle, even if we feel otherwise. That is His promise to us.

God does not allow us to experience more than we can handle, even if we feel otherwise.

If you've lost a child, keep in mind that the more you allow others to support and care for you, the sooner you'll recover. Christians don't detour around grief. They do have greater resources available to handle it, however. Let others help you, pray for you, and love you. Tell your story as often as you need to. Listen to these comments from a survivor of a neonatal death and a support-group facilitator:

> Every time you talk about it, every time you go through your story and talk about some part of the grief process, as painful as

it might be at the moment, it becomes easier. Some people need to continue to talk about it a few times. Some people need to continue to talk about it over and over again. I felt the need for a long time to tell the story. At least a year.[12]

Recovery will not mean a once-and-for-all conclusion to your grief, especially with any loss regarding a child. It's a twofold process: (1) regaining your ability to function as you once did, and (2) resolving and integrating your loss into your life.

In a sense, however, you will never recover completely, because you'll never be exactly the way you were before. Your loss changes you. As someone once asked in a counseling session, "If I can't be the way I was before and I never recover completely, what is all this about recovery? I'm confused. What does it mean? How can you recover but not fully recover?"

Recovery means you get your capabilities and attributes back so you can use them. It means you reach a point where you're no longer fighting your loss but accepting it. Acceptance doesn't mean you would have chosen it or even that you like it, but you've learned to live with it as a part of your life. Recovery doesn't mean you don't mourn occasionally and watch out for holidays and special dates. It means you learn to go on with your life.

I still have a scar from an incision made during an operation when I was a child. It reminds me that I had that experience. Recovery is like a scar from an operation, but it's in such a sensitive place that on occasion you feel the ache again. You can't predict when it will happen. In writing this and the preceding chapter, the ache returned for me several times.

Recovering means reinvesting in life. A newfound source of joy is possible. But you could very well feel uncomfortable with whatever is new. You may think that experiencing the joys of life again is somehow wrong. Besides, if you begin to hope or trust again, you could experience another loss. I've talked to some people who never want another child or who distance themselves from the remaining children to protect themselves.

The Lord is the source of our joy. The psalmist stated that He "clothes us with joy." God extends to each of us the invitation to reinvest in life.[13]

I will exalt you, O Lord,

for you lifted me out of the depths
    and did not let my enemies gloat over me.
O LORD my God, I called to you for help
    and you healed me.
O LORD, you brought me up from the grave;
    you spared me from going down into the pit.
Sing to the LORD, you saints of his;
    praise his holy name.
For his anger lasts only a moment,
    but his favor lasts a lifetime;
weeping may remain for a night,
    but rejoicing comes in the morning.
When I felt secure, I said,
    "I will never be shaken."
O LORD, when you favored me,
    you made my mountain stand firm;
but when you hid your face,
    I was dismayed.
To you, O LORD, I called;
    to the Lord I cried for mercy:
    "What gain is there in my destruction,
    in my going down into the pit?
Will the dust praise you?
    Will it proclaim your faithfulness?
Hear, O LORD, and be merciful to me;
    O LORD, be my help."
You turned my wailing into dancing;
    you removed my sackcloth and clothed me with joy,
that my heart may sing to you and not be silent.
    O LORD my God, I will give you thanks forever. (Ps. 30)

Did you notice what that psalm said about grief and recovery?
In grief, we sometimes feel as if we're going to die.
In grief, we sometimes feel as if God has hidden His face.
In grief, we also have times when we feel God has favored us.
In recovery, we discover that weeping will not last forever!

What about you? Are there clothes of mourning that you would like to exchange for clothes of joy?

You don't usually have a choice in your loss, but you do have a choice in your recovery. The changes in your identity, relationships, new roles, and even abilities can be either positive or negative.

I have seen people who choose to live in denial and move ahead as though nothing has really happened. I have seen people stuck in the early stages of their grief who choose to lead lives of bitterness and blame. Some become so hardened and angry that it's difficult to be around them for long. They've made a choice. Life is full of losses, but you have the choice of doing something constructive or destructive with your loss. It's not the fault of other people or of God.

Are there any criteria you can use in the grieving process to evaluate whether recovery is occurring? Yes, there are. It often helps, however, to go through such an evaluation with a person who can give you an objective viewpoint.

Dr. Therese Rando has made an outstanding contribution to the study of grief and recovery.[14] She suggests that recovery should be seen by observing changes in yourself, in your relationship with what you lost, and in your relationship with the world and other people. As you read the following evaluation, the conclusions you reach may help you decide where you are in your recovery.

On a scale of 0 to 10 (0 meaning "not at all" and 10 meaning "total recovery in that area"), rate yourself in response to each question. This evaluation is geared toward the loss of a person, but it can be adapted to other losses as well.[15]

Changes in Myself Because of My Loss

I have returned to normal levels of functioning in most areas of my life.
0——————————————————5——————————————————10

My overall symptoms of grief have declined.
0——————————————————5——————————————————10

My feelings do not overwhelm me when I think about my loss or someone mentions it.

0————————————————5————————————————10

Most of the time, I feel all right about myself.

0————————————————5————————————————10

I enjoy myself and what I experience without feeling guilty.

0————————————————5————————————————10

My anger has diminished, and when it occurs, it is handled appropriately.

0————————————————5————————————————10

I don't avoid thinking about things that could be or are painful.

0————————————————5————————————————10

My hurt has diminished, and I understand it.

0————————————————5————————————————10

I can think of positive things.

0————————————————5————————————————10

I have completed what I need to do about my loss.

0————————————————5————————————————10

My pain does not dominate my thoughts or my life.

0————————————————5————————————————10

I can handle special days or dates without being totally overwhelmed by
memories.

0————————————————5————————————————10

I can remember the loss on occasion without pain and without crying.

0————————————————5————————————————10

There is meaning and significance to my life.

0———————————————5———————————————10

I am able to ask *how* rather than *why* at this time.

0———————————————5———————————————10

I see hope and purpose in life in spite of my loss.

0———————————————5———————————————10

I have energy and can feel relaxed during the day.

0———————————————5———————————————10

I no longer fight the fact that the loss has occurred. I have accepted it.

0———————————————5———————————————10

I am learning to be comfortable with my new identity and in being without what I lost.

0———————————————5———————————————10

I understand that my feelings over the loss will return periodically, and I
can accept that.

0———————————————5———————————————10

I understand what grief means and have a greater appreciation for it.

0———————————————5———————————————10

Changes in My Relationship with the Person I Lost

I remember our relationship realistically, with positive and negative memories.

0———————————————5———————————————10

My relationship with the person I lost is healthy and appropriate.

0———————————————5———————————————10

I feel all right about not thinking about the loss for a time. I am not betraying the one I lost.

0————————————————5————————————————10

I have a new relationship with the child I have lost. I know appropriate ways of keeping my child alive in my memories.

0————————————————5————————————————10

I no longer go on a search for my loved one.

0————————————————5————————————————10

I don't feel compelled to hang on to the pain.

0————————————————5————————————————10

The ways I keep my loved one alive are healthy and acceptable.

0————————————————5————————————————10

I can think about things in life other than what I lost.

0————————————————5————————————————10

My life has meaning even though this person is gone.

0————————————————5————————————————10

Changes I Have Made in Adjusting to My New World

I have integrated my loss into my world, and I can relate to others in a healthy way.

0————————————————5————————————————10

I can accept the help and support of other people.

0————————————————5————————————————10

I am open about my feelings in other relationships.

0————————————————5————————————————10

I feel it is all right for life to go on even though my loved one is gone.

0————————————————5————————————————10

I have developed an interest in people and things outside myself that have no relationship to the person I lost.

0————————————————5————————————————10

I have put the loss in perspective.

0————————————————5————————————————10

Isaiah said that God "shall be the stability of your times" (Isa. 33:6, NASB). His presence in our lives will enable us to recover.

Seven

Your Marriage and the Other Children

*F*OREST FIRE! The words elicit fear in the hearts of all who live in richly timbered areas. When a fire erupts, the best strategy is to confront it immediately and contain it. Equipment is brought in with appropriate manpower, and one of the first tasks is to construct firebreaks so the fire doesn't spread. Sometimes those firebreaks work. But when they don't, the fire fighters' efforts are taken away from the heart of the blaze to try to stop the new outbreak, and the time involved in quenching the fire is extended.

A crisis with a child isn't much different. If it were your only difficulty and it could be contained to just that, life would be easier. But what's happening with your child affects your marriage and your other children as well. It doesn't have to be a negative legacy, however. It can become a tremendous time of growth.

Strains and Stresses

What happens to the marriage relationship? Extra strains and stresses will be placed on it. Many marriages break up over the birth and care of a disabled child or the death of a child. Why? Many factors contribute, but if

– 105 –

the relationship was fragile to begin with, the difficulty with a child could be the crushing blow.

Dr. Rosemarie Cook suggests that the following variables will affect the marriage:

- the individuals themselves, what they bring of their past into the marriage
- the stability and strength of the individuals
- the maturity level of the individuals
- the strength of the relationship before the child was born
- the health, educational, and financial circumstances of the couple
- the number, ages, and gender of other children in the family
- the strength of the faith of the couple
- the social supports for the family
- the community services that will help care for the child[1]

One factor affecting the relationship is emotional separation. After the discovery of a rebellious child or the diagnosis of a child with a disability, the couple are often so focused on the problem that they don't

> *Ironically, perhaps, a close marital relationship can create additional stresses.*

even share a cup of coffee or a meal. If they do sit down together, their discussion centers on the problem and rarely on themselves. And when two people can't find comfort and emotional support with each other, they may find ways to numb their pain instead of working through it. Frequently, either another person or excessive involvement in outside activities becomes the substitute.

Ironically, perhaps, a close marital relationship can create additional stresses. The strength of the relationship can make you vulnerable to the blame and anger that grievers often displace onto those nearest to them. And because of your closeness, you not only feel your own pain and grief, but also those of your spouse. The empathy so important in a quality marriage is now a conduit for more pain. This often makes it difficult to have any rest or relief. You may be fearful of asking for time out from the stress because of your concern for your partner.

When the grief is severe (as in the death of a child) or ongoing (as with a disabled or rebellious child), your security, strength, assertiveness, independence, and health are all under attack. Normal differences and marital friction may be blown out of proportion because of the energy drain caused by preoccupation with the crisis. Some of the common problems are:

• One partner keeps asking the other those unanswerable questions: "Why? Why did this happen? Why us? Why did God let this happen? Why? Why? Why?"

• One partner avoids talking with the other because of exhaustion, emotional distance, or concern that it might make things worse for him or her.

• One partner makes irrational demands, such as asking the other to have answers, fix the problem, or take away the pain.

• One partner makes rational but unrealistic demands, such as asking the other to do tasks for which the person is unsuited or to take over the duties of both.

These and other communication problems will push couples further apart. An underlying, if often unadmitted, fear is of losing other family members (such as your spouse) at this time, and any communication problems fuel the fear.[2]

Differences in Grieving

We tend to assume that when there's a loss in the family, everyone grieves in the same way and at the same pace. That's far from the truth, however, for we all grieve in a personal way. Each person has suffered a different loss, since each person in the family had a unique relationship with the child. The different roles and relationships, as well as the amount of time spent with the child, will affect grieving.

In the case of a stillborn or a disabled newborn, the losses will affect more of your hopes and expectations. Seeing the football and the baseball glove purchased prior to birth now sitting in the disabled child's room, never to be used, may affect the athletic father more than the mother. If you waited for children until your mid-thirties and then had a Down's syndrome baby, your hopes for other children may enter the world of loss. Or having one child for whom you held high hopes for academic achievement may lead to a major loss when he drops out of high school and then is arrested for selling drugs.

You and your spouse won't grieve the same way, either, for men and women do it differently. We expect this, unfortunately. A man will talk about the facts—"My son dropped out of school"—rather than his feelings—"I'm so disappointed with him. At times I just feel depressed and wonder if it was worth all the time and effort." After a while, a man becomes silent about his loss. His grief seems to decline more rapidly, which can lead his wife to feel he doesn't care as much about the problem or the child. (Chapter 9 deals more fully with men and their grief.)

You also won't be synchronized in your grief in the sense that when one of you is stabilized, the other will be down, and vice versa. Other differences include the following:

• *How you express feelings.* One may want to talk, while the other doesn't. If one tends to be talkative anyway and the partner is quiet, the difference may be intensified at this time. Which feelings are expressed could also be an issue: One sheds tears of sorrow, and the other declares strong words of anger and protest.

• *How you face work and daily activities.* Often one person is immobilized by the crisis and the new set of responsibilities. But for the other, work and activities are a welcome relief.

• *How you relate to things that bring back memories.* Photographs and mementos of enjoyable times with a child who is now rebellious or has died may be a source of conflict. One wants them in constant view, and the other wants them out of sight. With a disabled child, one parent may still want to buy certain items, while the other sees no need for them.

• *How you react to the other children.* One parent may seek more involvement with the child, maintain a normal level of involvement and share his grief, or withdraw to protect the child from his own grief. Whichever direction that parent chooses, the other is likely doing something else.

The problems here may multiply, because the child may want something entirely different from the parent.

• *How you seek support from others.* One may want to reach out to friends or a support group, while the other may not want any contact.

• *How you respond sexually to each other.* When a child dies, sexual relations can be affected for up to two years. The fear of having and losing another child and guilt over experiencing pleasure are common issues. To avoid further hurt, you may want to avoid intimacy. And often the one wanting sexual involvement has difficulty understanding why the other is

When you listen to each other, hear what your spouse has difficulty putting into words.

avoiding it. This may be something that both need but one cannot handle. The level of physical exhaustion and mental energy drain also mitigates against sexual interest.

• *How you respond to living your life as you had been.* One wants to continue with life as it used to be because it helps to control the pain. But the other finds that carrying on the usual routine and socializing produce guilt. It feels like a betrayal. Sometimes with a rebellious child, one parent wants life to go on to let the child know that what he or she has done isn't going to get the family down.

• *How you respond to your Christian faith.* It can draw you together or become a wedge between you. Some learn to rely even more on the Lord and find the comfort promised by Scripture, but the spouse may feel that God has let the family down and want nothing to do with Him.[3]

Keeping the Marriage Strong

To avoid having these issues hinder their marriage, couples can take several steps to minister to themselves and to each other.

1. Set a regular time each day to talk about events and share both thoughts and feelings. Make it a private time, just for the two of you, and eliminate any possible interruptions before you begin.

2. When you listen to each other, hear what your spouse has difficulty putting into words. Reflect back what you think or feel your spouse could be experiencing. If your mate is struggling with some issue, don't attempt to "fix it" unless asked to do so. Just listening is often assistance enough.

3. Agree on family activities that will always be shared by both spouses, even though you would rather the other person took sole responsibility for them. Agree also on activities that each can do without relying on the other.

Make it a point to go on a date together each week, whether you feel like it or not. And when you do, put a gag rule on what you discuss; concentrate on talking about issues other than the difficulty with your child. You need private time together to nurture your relationship. No matter how strapped we were financially—and for a number of years things were very tight—we decided to never debate whether we had money for a baby-sitter for Matthew. Those dates were a survival necessity for us.

4. In addition to together time, each of you will need solitary time. Encourage one another to do this rather than resisting it. Trade off so that one shoulders the parenting for a while. One wife told me the 15 minutes a day her husband gave her as his gift were worth more than anything else he did (sometimes it was a half hour).

Her husband even drew a bubble bath for her and placed her novel next to it for her to read. She said this daily ritual turned her into a new woman. Sometimes couples do trade-offs for each other for half a day each Saturday.[4]

The Other Children

Whenever there's a loss of any kind with a child in the family, the siblings are affected, too. They have a greater-than-usual level of neediness. They want more nurturing from their parents at a time when their parents have less to give.

If your family has suffered such a loss, your other children may be having a difficult time while your energy is directed toward coping with the rebelling child, mourning the death of a child, or trying to discover the exact condition of your disabled child. Often the other children struggle with guilt because they are "normal" while their sibling isn't, or they're alive and their sibling is dead. Worse yet, they may feel that something they said, did, or even felt may have created the problem.

Too often when a crisis arises, no one thinks about talking to the other children about what's going on and why. Consequently, they continue to struggle with their feelings, questions, and pain. They may feel alone and even quite angry. They may respond in many ways, especially if they feel neglected.

You may not see much of a noticeable change in your child. Or you may see a very positive change as a child decides to be overly good as her means of survival. She makes few demands on her exhausted and stressed parents, and she tries to be helpful. But she, too, has needs her parents have to meet, and she also requires an opportunity to grieve.

Many children hide their distress and have to deal with it years later, in adulthood. But another common reaction is to employ attention-getting mechanisms when their sibling is rebelling, and especially if the child is disabled. It's the only way they know to recapture their parents' attention. And if their attempts are ignored or discounted, they could intensify their efforts in this direction by using drugs, running away, setting fires, destroying property, and so on. Expressed anger is one way to gain attention.[5]

Children raised with a disabled sibling often feel a strong sense of responsibility, either self-imposed or placed there by their parents. Dr. Charlotte Thompson tells the story of a pediatrician who grew up with a disabled sibling. The family knew something was wrong with her brother, but the problem wasn't diagnosed until he was 15. He wasn't expected to do chores or have outside jobs like the other children. The parents had time and money for him, but very little for the others. They put up with temper tantrums and angry explosions from him, but they wouldn't tolerate any expression of anger from the others.

The disabled child knew he was favored and used it to his advantage. He ended up being viewed as the good child and the others as the bad ones.

Finally, the problem was diagnosed and a tumor was removed, but by then the family's finances were depleted. During that time, the other children never voiced their concern over the unfairness. When this pediatrician was in counseling for her marriage, her therapist told her,

You've been carrying your brother on your back all of your life, which is probably one of the reasons you went into pediatrics. You have been trying to understand what happened with your brother and why you always felt him around your neck like a millstone. You have a highly overdeveloped sense of responsibility toward other children and have tried to mother the world. This has caused emotional problems, marital problems, and has left you feeling drained, angry, and incomplete. Essentially you have had to be your own parent, and after your parents died, you felt a tremendous responsibility for your brother. By transferring his dependence from your parents to you, you created a very difficult problem for yourself. You may well know that people often grow to dislike, or even hate, close individuals on whom they feel dependent. This surely was your brother's case. First he hated your parents, and now he hates you.[6]

That situation could have been avoided if the parents had communicated with the other children and they had all worked together as a team. But who ever helps parents deal with their grief and gives them guidelines for responding to the other children? Usually no one does, which is why you need the assistance of other parents who have gone through the same struggles.

You may be aware that you're not doing what you want or need to with the other children. Your grief drains your energy and the emotional investment you want to make in them. So you feel you're not being the parent you want to be, which adds to your frustration and sense of failure. But during the onset of the crisis with your child, it's unrealistic to think you can act the way you want with the other children. You just don't have enough to give.

You will also fluctuate in your feelings and responses to your children. You may feel resentment that your other children are healthy or still living, don't seem to be as concerned or grieving enough, or have adjusted too soon. Part of your response is your anger over the unfairness of what has happened. You may feel you can't invest what you want or you've lost your ability to give. Or you may be afraid to invest because something bad could happen to these children. You could also overreact and over-protect. Being aware of these difficulties may help you to avoid them.[7]

Research has provided us with helpful information about what to expect and what might be avoided.

- Older siblings adjust better than younger children do to having a brother or sister with disabilities, with the exception of the eldest daughter, who doesn't adjust as well.
- Eldest daughters often are given the task of caring for the child with special needs, much more often than are any other children in the family.
- Children are more affected by having a sibling with a disability if that sibling is of the same gender.
- If there are only two children in the family and if the non-disabled sibling is a girl, she suffers more adverse effects.
- If there are only two children in the family and one has a disability, the other is more pressured to fulfill the parents' hopes and dreams for success in their children. If the non-disabled child is a girl, she is also assigned more caregiving responsibility.
- Siblings of children with disabilities tend to show positive qualities of being well-adjusted, mature beyond their years, tolerant of differences in people, helpful toward people, and aware of social needs.
- Siblings can be excellent teachers of their brothers and sisters with disabilities because they are in a different position in the family.
- Siblings may judge the worth of their friends by the friends' reactions to their brother or sister with the disability.
- Siblings may experience guilt as they surpass a disabled younger brother or sister in skills and abilities.
- The siblings may feel pressure to overachieve.
- Siblings may overidentify with a mildly disabled brother or sister or may, as they reach teen years, not consider a severely disabled sibling a person.
- Siblings may feel that requests by parents for help with the brother or sister with a disability are an intrusion on their

time, or they may view it as a privilege to cooperate with the parents.[8]

It's interesting that choosing a helping profession as a vocation is common among the siblings of disabled people. Sometimes the other children carry guilt, feelings of responsibility, or a sense of chronic sorrow or sadness into adulthood. Sometimes the acceptance of a disabled brother or sister gets harder as kids grow older. As a daughter of some friends put it, "I grow older and change. But my sister stays the same, and at times it seems as though she goes backward. She's an adult like I am, but I'm a real adult, and she's still in infancy. And she always will be. That's sad."

Siblings face numerous pressures that we don't even think about. What does a child say to others when asked about a younger brother who just died?

What does a child say to others when asked about an older sister who is on drugs and has just become pregnant?

What does a child say to others when asked about a sibling who doesn't look disabled in any way but is nonverbal?

Sometimes the *less severe* the impairment, the more difficult it is for the siblings, since they may feel embarrassed about their brother's or sister's behavior.

Matthew and Sheryl

We wondered how Matthew affected our daughter, Sheryl. She seemed to handle his presence all right, but we weren't always sure. We remembered various incidents over the years. One day when Matthew was very young, Sheryl was at a neighbor's house where they had a baby three months younger than Matthew. That baby was turning over and sitting up. Sheryl came home and asked why their baby was able to do those things and Matthew wasn't, even though he was older. When Joyce told her that Matthew was slower and wouldn't be able to for a while, Sheryl didn't say anything, but the hurt was visible on her face.

As Sheryl grew older, she never hid from the fact that her brother was mentally retarded. She never shielded the fact from her friends. We wondered if she would be embarrassed about it, but she would bring her friends home, and when they met Matthew she would casually say, "This is my brother, Matthew. He's retarded." Then she would go on with what she was doing. Her friends were the ones who didn't seem to know how to respond.

As Sheryl moved through junior and senior high school, we noticed that she seemed to be sensitive to the needs of other retarded people and protective if others mistreated them.

Just recently I talked with Sheryl, who at the time of this writing is 31. I asked her how Matthew affected her and what problems she experienced in having a disabled brother.

"I don't think of any problems I had with Matthew being retarded when I was young," she said. "I didn't feel left out in any way. In fact, my first memory of Matthew was when Grandma and I were taking him for a stroll around the block and he had a seizure. Grandma became very upset. I went to a house, knocked on the door, told the lady that my brother was having a seizure, and asked to borrow a spoon. The lady and I held him and used the spoon in his mouth so he wouldn't choke. I wasn't upset. It made me feel like I was really a part of the family since I could help him.

"When I was young, his condition didn't bother me. It was like riding in an airplane or going through an earthquake when I was a child. I didn't fully understand the significance and all the ramifications of those situations, nor of retardation. When I became an adult I understood, and then it was difficult to deal with. I couldn't handle going to Matthew's home and seeing all the other disabled children. It just tore me to pieces. I have a difficult time seeing retarded children now."

After Sheryl said that, we talked a bit more. I told her that I understood and have a similar response and sensitivity to seeing anyone with a disability. It took me years to discover that what I was feeling was the wish that I could reach out and heal that person—make him or her whole— followed by the frustration of knowing I couldn't.

Sheryl floored me with her response: "I don't think Matthew's retardation was something for us to try to heal. I think his purpose was to bring healing to all of us. We're all different because of him. I know I'm a different person because of Matthew."

I just stood there silently, letting the truth of her profound statement sink in. Her words left me with nothing to say. My tears were the only response I could make. When she came across the room to hug me, I told her that was one of the most special things she had ever said.

How You Can Help

What can you do to help your children? Give uninterrupted time to each child, and listen to his or her concerns. This is valuable not only for your child, but it will also help you shift your focus from the crisis or problem to the normal affairs of life. We all need an occasional break from the crisis. Explain the situation, as well as what to expect in the future, to each child according to his or her level of understanding.

Perhaps the most helpful step you can take (although a difficult one because of what you're experiencing yourself) is to help your other children grieve and handle the loss from their perspective. They grieve as you do, but they'll manifest it differently. Too often, parents assume their other children don't understand or are not that affected by the crisis, but that's not true. You can't protect your children from their own pain in a family crisis. Fathers are especially prone to try to "rescue" the other children.

In the case of a child who is rebelling, the siblings could be struggling with disappointment, anger over the disruption in the family, grief over personal losses associated with a broken relationship with their sibling, or tension over conflicting loyalties to their parents and their sibling.

With a disabled sibling, the grief could be over the loss of the relationship they expected or of the routine of the household.

When a child dies, the siblings struggle with many factors in addition to their grief. They will live longer with the death than the parents will. They are now very aware that they, too, can die. Sometimes they struggle with guilt over their relationship with the deceased child and your inability to prevent the death. Their emotional turmoil is a combination of their grief and yours. You need to be aware of any of their attempts to take away your pain by being perfect for you or trying to be a replacement.[9]

Children are not nearly as equipped as adults to handle loss, especially when it involves a family member. Their thinking processes are immature. They have few experiences from which to draw, lack the vocabulary to describe their thoughts and feelings, and take things literally. For instance, if you tell your kids that you have lost someone close to you, they may assume the person will be found again.

Parents need to identify anything that may inhibit a child's ability to grieve the loss of a sibling. These are some of the most common obstacles:

• The parents have difficulty grieving past or current losses and have not provided a model.

> *Children are not nearly as equipped as adults to handle loss, especially when it involves a family member.*

• The parents are unable to handle their children's expression of painful experiences.

• The children worry about how the parents are handling the loss and try to protect them.

• The children are overly concerned with maintaining control and feeling secure and may be frightened or threatened by their grief. The feelings may be too intense.

• The children do not have the security of a loving, caring environment.

• The parents do not caringly stimulate and encourage the children to grieve.

• In the case of a sibling's death, children may question their role in making it happen. This misplaced guilt is further enhanced if they have ambivalent feelings toward the sibling.

• The family fails to acknowledge and discuss the reality of death or other loss.

Regardless of the type of loss your family has experienced, the following steps will help your children to grieve:

1. Children need to accept the loss, experience the pain, and express their sorrow. Encourage them to talk about their feelings. Draw them out.

2. Children require assistance to identify and express the wide range of feelings they're experiencing. Give them permission to cry, to feel sad and lonesome. Be a caring listener.

3. In the case of death, kids need encouragement to remember and review their relationship with their sibling. Looking at pictures and videos and recalling activities together are important.

4. Children need help in learning to relinquish and say good-bye to what they have lost, whether it be a sibling who dies or their hopes and relationship with a disabled or rebelling sibling.

5. Remember that each child responds differently to loss, depending on age and level of emotional maturity.

The younger the children, the more they grieve intermittently. They don't have your capacity to tolerate the pain of a loss for a long time, so they mourn for a while, play for a while, mourn for a while, and so on.

And kids who experience the death of a sibling can experience a number of fears, including the following:

• Fear of losing parents, other siblings, or grandparents. They tend to see the remaining people as candidates for death.

• Fear of their own death, especially if they were younger than a sibling who died and they're approaching the age at which he or she died. If there was a disabling accident, they may become concerned as they approach that age.

• Fear of going to sleep because they equate sleep with death. Even the prayer "If I should die before I wake ..." reinforces this misconception. Dreams and nightmares intensify the fear.

• Fear of separation because of the perceived insecurity of the home and family. They no longer feel protected but fear that anything could happen. And they're hesitant to talk about their feelings because they may upset other family members.

Another problem associated with grief is guilt. There seem to be three main reasons children experience guilt when they suffer a loss:

1. "She died (or left or was disabled) because I did something wrong. I misbehaved!"

Children have a knack for remembering things they've done that they think were wrong. They may have made a mistake, broken something, or forgotten to say or do something. Just like adults, they can end up with an incredible list of "if onlys" or regrets.

2. "I wanted him dead. I thought it, and it happened."

Young children believe they can actually make things happen by thinking them. It's easy for kids to think their anger or aggression killed their brother, for example, or made him the way he is. Because they take on this responsibility, they live in fear of being found out and punished.

3. "I didn't love her enough."

Children believe that loving someone enough will keep the person from dying. They long for a second chance to make things right.

One other common grief response is anger. A number of beliefs trigger children's anger. They often feel abandoned and left to face life on their own. They're angry because their future has been dramatically changed—they won't be with that special brother or sister anymore. I've seen younger children very angry with older siblings because of the chaos their rebellion created.[10] (For additional help, see *Kids Have Feelings Too,* by Gary Oliver and Norm Wright [Victor Books].)

Your marriage and your other children don't have to be secondary casualties of the original crisis. You can take steps to strengthen your marriage and family life, and then you'll have a greater source of strength to draw from as you confront the issues facing you. As your family works, plays, and worships together, you will discover a healing comfort in these relationships. Be sure you allow the other family members to minister to you as you minister to them.

Eight

Families That Make It

CHANGE is inevitable when a crisis invades your family. Do you want to be a victim of the direction that change takes, or do you want to be in charge of it? You have a choice.

Strong words? Yes. True words? Yes. If you've already experienced your crisis, you know what I'm saying. Some families draw closer and become more compassionate. Others become splintered and soon disintegrate.

We've seen them. When Matthew lived at Salem Christian Home, 20 children with multiple disabilities occupied his unit. Only a few of their families were intact. Most had fragmented.

Many families, instead of working out solutions for their pain and problems, begin to attack each other in the months following a crisis, whether it be the birth of a disabled child, the discovery of a child's disability, a death, or a child's rebellion. And if conflicts have been buried for years, the restraints are usually lifted at this time, and they erupt. So the family has to deal not only with the crisis itself, but also with the unresolved conflicts. Each drains energy needed for the others.

A family works together as a system or large body. Each person is part of it. When the body loses an arm (as in a death), is permanently injured (as in a disabled child), or has one part refuse to cooperate with the rest and do its own thing (as in a rebellious child), all the other parts are affected. They have to learn to adjust and, sometimes, assume new roles.

It's similar to an old-fashioned balance scale. If something is added to one side, it alters the other side by the same amount in the opposite direction. If the scale is ever to be balanced again, something has to be added to one side or subtracted from the other.

Your family is like that scale. The members have to adjust to handle the change and get back into balance. Many aspects of family life—including power, responsibilities, and roles—may need to be reassigned. The longer the central individual was in the family or the greater the significance of his or her position (such as the oldest child rebelling), the more adjustments will have to be made.

I've seen cases in which one child committed serious offenses that drew attention away from the parents' marital problems. But when the child was jailed and no longer there, the problems became apparent, and another child began to be the troublemaker to ease the marital tensions. In some families, when a disabled child is placed in a permanent outside residence, other issues that had gone unnoticed begin to surface.

Between the time a loss occurs and the individual family members discover their new roles and stabilize, there's a time of uncertainty and turmoil. Because of the reality of the loss, it's difficult to make some of the necessary changes. Each family member needs time and space to deal with the loss in his or her own way. It may take a while for each one to find his or her new role, especially following a death. You'll feel like a juggler at times, trying to deal with your own needs and still be helpful to the other family members.

After a crisis hits, you'll also have to weigh the needs of a particular family member against the needs of the family as a whole. You'll have to work for a balance. What do you do, for example, when a child dies or runs away close to Christmas? How do you respond when some want to get a Christmas tree and celebrate Christmas and some don't?[1]

Potential Problems

Whenever a crisis involves a child, you need to be aware of the tendency to create a "replacement child." Sometimes surviving children are expected to meet parental needs left vacant by the child. This can create severe emotional problems. In some extreme cases, parents decide either to have or to adopt another child to take the place of the one who died or rebelled. It's as though they want another opportunity to succeed or fulfill their needs. But you cannot re-create a lost or wayward child.

Parents also tend to become overprotective or overly strict with remaining children. You want to ensure that what happened to your other child doesn't happen to them. But as you try to draw these children closer through restriction and confinement, you're probably pushing them further away. They could learn to resent you and end up being estranged—the very situation you didn't want.

As mentioned earlier, you may struggle if your other children don't respond to the crisis the way you do or think they should. You could resent them because they seem to have adjusted too quickly or don't realize the seriousness of what happened.

Families that cope well with heartbreaks and crisis have specific characteristics, as do those that don't handle them well. Let's consider first the families that cope poorly.

Most of these families are not prepared for life's setbacks. They survive well when things are going well. Some people actually deny the possibility that crises could happen to them. When others experience divorce, death, unemployment, or illness, they seldom have any empathy. I've talked with people attending my "Recovering from Loss" seminars who have difficulty identifying any major losses in their lives.

One man said, "Norm, I just can't relate to any of these experiences people are describing. What does that say about me? Is this a problem in my life?"

"How would you handle it if you experienced some major crisis or tragedy?" I asked. "What would you do?"

He paused for a moment and then said, "I don't know. I've never thought about it. I guess I never thought it would happen to me."

Unfortunately, too many people believe it just happens to others, not to them.

A second characteristic of families that don't cope well is that *they frequently hurt one another by keeping silent.* It's a challenge, but interaction among family members is vital. Often, however, they retreat into their own inner worlds and don't express their thoughts or feelings. Or within a family, some want to talk, but others don't. The family may not communicate at critical times because they never learned to talk when everything was going well. People aren't likely to have the energy, time, and capability to learn communication skills when life is falling apart around them.

Most people don't realize that the silent person(s) has power over other family members. For those who want to talk, the silence adds to the pressure of the crisis, and they also end up feeling rejected. Silence is a characteristic of dysfunctional families; it destroys and deadens hope.

> *People aren't likely to have the energy, time, and capability to learn communication skills when life is falling apart around them.*

And as the silence progresses, estrangement and frustration increase, which soon develop into another characteristic of noncoping families—blame.

Blame is one of the most significant characteristics of these families. None of us likes being out of control and left hanging. There has to be some closure to discovering what created the problem in the first place. If we have an explanation for what happened, we can understand it better, handle it better, and feel relieved that someone else was at fault. The more serious the crisis, the greater we feel the need to discover the cause. Statements that start with "If only you had or hadn't . . ." or "Why didn't you or did you . . ." begin to fly from one person to another, and if a family member knows the other people's areas of vulnerability, the accusations can get vicious.

You may not want to blame the others. Logically, blaming doesn't make sense. But good sense doesn't often prevail at this time. Rather, the surge of emotional turmoil and struggle for a reason for the difficulty become uppermost.

Because everyone is vulnerable at this time, accusations and other comments penetrate deep into the mind and heart of the receiver and will be remembered for years. No one wants to be unfairly accused or blamed. In the book of Proverbs we read, "There are those who speak rashly like the piercing of a sword" (12:18, AMPLIFIED), and "In a multitude of words transgression is not lacking" (10:19, AMPLIFIED). These verses reflect clearly the pain of unfair accusations.

A better approach is to follow the guidance of these passages: "Pleasant words are as a honeycomb, sweet to the mind and healing to the body" (16:24, AMPLIFIED); and "A word fitly spoken and in due season is like apples of gold in a setting of silver" (25:11, AMPLIFIED).

Another common characteristic of families that don't cope well is *magnifying the seriousness of their problems.* They take them to the extreme as they discuss them and imagine the worst possible consequences instead of being hopeful or waiting to see what the actual results will be. They interact too much—and in the wrong direction. When they discuss only their crises amongst themselves, without outside, objective assistance, they easily become overly pessimistic.

Coping Well

Many families, however, make it through their crises. They don't just survive; they grow. A crisis can activate emotional, intellectual, and spiritual resources that have lain dormant and never been called on before. Most of us want to belong to a cohesive, strong, and loving family. What are such families like?

First, *they don't allow themselves to be bitter.* They refuse to live in the past or permit the situation to stop their lives where they are and never look to the future. Bitterness comes from focusing on the unfairness of whatever has happened. It's like a warplane's radar locking onto a target but never letting go. It turns into resentment, and the bitter person becomes its victim.

Many of the people I've seen who were stuck in their grief were there because of holding on to resentment. In their minds, they built a wall around their bitterness. They didn't face it or allow it to drain. The resentment may have been against God, against the doctors, against the driver of the car that hit their son and left him in a coma, against their partners for what they did or didn't do, against the child who was into drugs and disruptive, or against themselves. But in each case, they injured themselves and hindered their own growth more than anyone else's.

Sometimes in discussing this situation, counselees will say, "Don't tell *me* to forgive them! I'm not about to, and they don't deserve it!"

They're surprised to hear me reply, "I'm not going to ask you to forgive them. You won't, you can't, and now is not the time. You're too hooked into what has happened. I would much rather work to help you get rid of that tremendous load of pain you're carrying around. Do you realize you've made a choice to allow yourself to be controlled emotionally by what happened and who was involved?"

The natural response of anger and resentment causes pain, to be sure. And too often we choose to let it stay in our lives and gain a foothold. I suggest a daily exercise of writing a letter (which you don't mail) to either the event itself or the person involved. Write as much as you can each time under two headings: "I resent . . ." and then "I wish . . ." In time, the bitterness will lift, and that's the first step in letting forgiveness have an opportunity to be expressed.

A similar problem that will keep a person and the entire family stuck in the past is the attitude of resignation: "I give up. Why try? Nothing will change. This will always be the problem." You believe you're defeated already, so you don't give God much room to work in the crisis or your heart. There were times when I wondered about our daughter, *How long will this go on? It's been three years now!*

Sometimes resignation is reflected in martyrdom. Martyrs complain inwardly and sulk, have a low-grade depression, or complain to just about everyone they meet about their difficulties. Unfortunately, in time this attitude will push others away.

A second characteristic of families that cope is that *they live in the present and have a future perspective.* They seek to learn from what has happened and not reside with regrets. They also learn to view the future not as threatening but as an opportunity. Most of the opportunities that will arise are completely unknown to you at the time.

As our pastor, Dr. Lloyd Ogilvie, said,

> The sure sign that we have an authentic relationship with God is that we believe more in the future than in the past. God gra-

ciously divided our life into days and years so that we could let go of yesterdays and anticipate our tomorrows. For our tomorrows, He gives us the gift of expectation and excitement.[2]

Holding on to the truth of Scripture and its promises will help a family cope. God said, "Do not be terrified; do not be discouraged, for the LORD your God will be with you wherever you go" (Josh. 1:9). He promised, "For I know the plans I have for you, . . . plans to prosper you and not to harm you, plans to give you hope and a future" (Jer. 29:11).

I was enthralled by a very different example of looking to the future and finding hope. In *A Gift of Hope*, Robert Veninga describes it:

Sometimes a family member will present a symbolic gift and in so doing protect the family from a sense of hopelessness. If you were to walk through the corridors of a children's hospital on Christmas Eve, *you would find rooms filled with symbolic gifts.* You might see a bicycle given to a child who will walk again only if he is willing to undergo hours of painful therapy. *Or you might find a sled given to a child* who has barely enough strength to make it to the bathroom. Or you might see a severely diabetic youngster learning to master Monopoly even though her eyesight is beginning to fail.

The cynic might ask what the utility of such gifts is, particularly if the boy can no longer walk or the girl can no longer see.

But each gift is given in hope. Its symbolic value far outweighs its utility. For when the child receives the bike, he can envision himself hustling over to a friend's house. When the sled is propped up in the hospital room, it is a symbol that life will not always be spent with needles and diagnostic tests. When a Monopoly game is mastered by sight, there is a recognition that it can be played when the eyes fail.

When a family member presents a symbolic gift or quietly expresses optimism, it has a powerful effect on the entire family. Sometimes all it takes is the image of that loved one to engender a sense of confidence in the future.[3]

Look to the future, and let it guide what you do now. Develop perseverance, for it's essential to keeping a family going, to working through a death or an ongoing crisis. Sometimes the family tensions are the worst experience.

Resolving Conflict

A third characteristic of families that cope is that *they learn to manage and resolve their conflicts*. Families that don't do this heap one conflict upon another. And when a new one occurs, they respond to it out of the contamination of all the unresolved issues in their reservoir. If you haven't learned to resolve conflicts before a crisis, you're not likely to do it during one.

When family members know conflicts aren't resolved, some may take

A *healthy family overrides its fears and discovers ways to make things different.*

the attitude of "Why even bother?" and not listen or engage others in conversation. A healthy family overrides its fears and discovers ways to make things different. Members learn to solve problems and are willing to listen to one another and try something new. This approach is a source of encouragement and hope in the midst of heartache.

It's also important to determine which problems are worth tackling, which are not, and which ones can be resolved. At times, you'll need to postpone problem solving or take time out.

Joan and Don are a good example of survival qualities in the midst of pain. They were in full-time ministry and had raised five children. But then their youngest daughter rebelled, became sexually active, and got pregnant. Their dreams for her were damaged, their relationship with her broken.

Their hopes for her future were put on hold, and their grandchild was adopted into another family. Then financial difficulties hit, forcing Don into another profession. Here's their story:

Joan shared her feelings:

I know one of the things that contributed to my healing was the decision to not keep what was happening to us a private matter. That was a hard decision because I grew up always wanting to help and please people. I wanted to make a difference in my world. To admit seeming failure, that I have a child who is going berserk according to my goals and values, was a difficult thing to let be known. I know I shared our story with some people who would rather have not known, but that's the chance you take. And once I shared openly that our daughter had left home, was living with a man, and was pregnant, I had a lot of people praying.

The comfort that I was willing to accept from God was part of my healing too. I could choose not to be comforted. I could find comfort in any number of things, but I have to *choose* to be comforted.

Don remembered:
Hillary and Chad were the first couple to call us and say, "Come on over for dinner." When their daughter had run away years before, I had thought, *Why is she teaching in a Christian school when she has a kid who behaves this way?* I thought somewhat less of Chad too. I assumed they blew it someplace along the line. Now I say, "Hey, we're one of them!" Hillary and Chad were just wonderful and they helped us begin to heal.

Joan and I were tough. We had been raised in the midwest mindset: "Never admit you hurt." Well, we did hurt, and we hurt deeply. I had a friend who was going through the same thing at the same time, and he and I got together every noon for months and prayed. Finally we began to heal as we realized we had done everything we knew how. I'm sure we made mistakes raising all of our kids, but we did what we thought was right.

For the first few weeks, my wife and I didn't want to go to church. Now I can go to church and I don't worry what others think. I know I'm healing because I don't even think about what they're thinking of me.

When our daughter was still home and doing the wrong

things, our counselor told Joan and me that we had to agree. We had to be one in how we dealt with her. I would say, "Well, we ought to do this to her as punishment," and Joan would say, "No, we can't do that." As the dad, it seemed I was always the tough guy and Joan always fixed things up. It really helped us to heal when we stopped fighting each other and began to agree on our actions.

We were finally able to release our daughter to the Lord because we saw more happen when we prayed than from listening to all the advice in the world. The support from friends was great. We needed their support.

But now it seems like we don't have the support that we did when we were in the midst of our problem. Actually, we're *still* in the midst of it. The baby is born and has been adopted, but our daughter isn't reconciled to God or to our family. I know, though, that God does hear and answer our prayers. One day we're going to see our daughter come back. I don't think I've experienced the death of a dream; it's just been delayed and altered. We're still in the process, but we have peace.

Joan shared her letting go experience:

I have had to let go of the visual pictures of our daughter and what she might have been. Someday she may still be some of that, but she will never be the young innocent girl she was in my dreams.

I had to allow God to change my perspective on what the future could be for our daughter. I always say, "Lord, anything You want," and then I present Him with this rigid little plan that I want Him to implement. I have received encouragement in letting Him redirect our lives when I think of a person like Chuck Colson. He could never be what he is today except for what he went through. When I think of how God is using people like Chuck Colson today, I get excited about what the future might be for our daughter.

Don commented:

I am seeing how faithful God is. Every knothole I go through, I see He is faithful. I almost look forward to what is going to happen next so I can see God's faithfulness. He stretches our character and our vision. We are learning to say, "Thank You, Lord," in advance because sometimes in the middle of it, you can't.[4]

Successful families believe each person has the ability to handle the adversity. They don't suffocate one another with "You should . . ." or "You ought to . . ." or by being overbearing with advice. Rather, they encourage one another. Unconditional love is the backbone for their relationships.

Personality differences are respected, too. If a person needs to talk or do something—or if the need is for privacy and quiet—that's all right.

The Power of Encouragement

Never underestimate the power of encouragement. It was illustrated beautifully a few years ago in a small midwestern town.

Crowds lined both sides of the street, all eyes peering in the same direction. Many people had been waiting for over an hour. Finally, in the distance, they saw a tiny speck moving slowly but steadily along the road. In another minute, the speck had grown. The people began to clap and cheer when they could make out the shape of a person propelling his wheelchair by hand. The cheering intensified as the smiling marathoner reached the edge of town.

The courageous paraplegic was traveling from one end of the country to the other. At a reception for him later that day, someone asked, "What keeps you going? Why go through all the pain and agony of pushing yourself day after day on those highways? How do you do it?"

He replied simply, "Didn't you hear it?"

"Hear what?" the man asked.

"You heard what keeps me going when I came into town. All those people clapping and cheering. That's what does it. All those cheerleaders. They're my encouragement. They believe in me. And then I believe I can make it. We all need someone to believe in us."

A crucial function of the family is to encourage each other. The word *encour-*

age means "to inspire to continue on a chosen course; impart courage or confidence to; embolden, hearten." Scripture calls us to "encourage . . . edify . . . build up" (1 Thess. 5:11, AMPLIFIED). Everyone needs a dose of encouragement. Everyone needs a dose of courage.

Families that sail through the years without upsets and tragedies are the exception rather than the rule. Without encouragement, we would all fail.

Imagine that you had long anticipated the birth of your first child. Everything went according to plan. The delivery was normal and easy; your son was alert and healthy—except he had no arms. Your tiny baby was born with a rare disease called bilateral upper extremity amelia.

Can you imagine how you would feel? The shock! The fear! The concern! How can he survive or function? Won't he have to be taken care of the rest of his life? How will our family make it? Should we have any other children?

Without encouragement, we would all fail.

That's one family's true story. Sixteen years later, their tale was told in the *Los Angeles Times.*[5] The boy lives with his mother, stepfather, and two younger siblings. Not only did his family survive, but he displays incredible courage. At 16 years of age, he maintains a 3.5 grade point average and runs on the cross-country team. Even more amazingly, he learned to use an acetylene torch for welding—using just his feet. He learned to use scissors at the age of four, to dress himself, to swim, and to use a computer.

Encouragement and pulling together made the difference.

Families that cope also have family members who protect one another when needed. They don't always wait to be asked, either. They listen with their eyes and their ears.

The quality or characteristic that sums up all the others and more is having a common faith in Jesus Christ and learning to experience the strength and comfort that come from Scripture and then share them with family members.

Guidelines Worth Remembering

What about you and your family? What has helped you to handle your crisis? Have you identified the elements? Perhaps if you did, you could rely on them more and also share what you've learned with others. Families can survive. Here are some summary guidelines to assist you and your family:

1. When a crisis occurs with a child, the entire family experiences a period of upheaval as the comfortable patterns of transaction between its members are disrupted.

2. To establish new, successful patterns, family members must adjust roles and relationships with other members.

3. During the beginning weeks of grief, the individual needs of family members may disrupt the family's ability to function as a unit. This will occur in an on-again/off-again fashion with a disabled or rebellious child as you hit various upsets along the way.

4. Each family member's grief progresses to different levels at different times. Each needs to look beyond his or her own personal loss if understanding within the family is to be achieved.

5. Remember the necessity for a good balance between family togetherness and individual freedom.

6. Learn to respond to family members' needs without suffocating the needy person.

7. Be aware that too much dependence between family members can destroy the boundaries protecting individual growth.

8. Allow each person the opportunity to absorb the loss in his or her own way and time. Some talk, some are quiet, some withdraw, and some may be active.

9. Do not, however, let the walls between family members grow insurmountably high. Don't respect privacy at the cost of the necessary sharing of grief.

10. Realize that children (particularly the eldest child) might feel compelled to try to assume the role of the one who dies or rebels.

11. Protect your children from taking on inappropriate responsibility. They are not adults and shouldn't be expected to function as such.

12. Recognize that as children grow from one stage of maturation to

another, family relationships and boundaries must be redefined accordingly.

13. If you have made decisions for your family that aren't working as you hoped they might, try to correct them.

14. Focus on the goals you hope to achieve, and above all, let others minister to you.[6]

☙Nine☙

Fathers and Their Grief

Fathers are neglected. It's true. When grieving occurs, they're often neglected. How does a father grieve the loss of a child or the ongoing loss of a disabled family member? How does he deal with the kaleidoscope of responses to a child's choosing a different life-style? Are there gender differences in the way grief is experienced and handled? Definitely.

A father who expresses, releases, or works through his grief thoroughly is not typical; he's the exception. A man is less likely than a woman to cry about, talk about, or even appear to be concerned about his loss. He tends to assume responsibility for the way he is feeling and responding. In other words, he prefers to depend on himself. He usually doesn't reach out to other people or a support group. His way of dealing with grief is covert, while a woman's is usually quite overt.

Even though a father's grief may not show that much and appears to be over sooner than a mother's, the grief is very real, as are the pressures it creates. A problem arises if the grief doesn't show: Where does it end up? That's what we need to consider.

The way other people respond to a man during grief often reinforces his responses. Who usually receives the most concern and attention during the loss? The woman. There's normally someone caring or expressing concern for her, but not for the husband-father. I've heard men say, "What about me? No one seems to care what I'm going through!"[1]

A father who lost his child said,

> I was alone that weekend. Female friends came to visit Mary in
> the hospital. They hugged her, talked to her, allowed her to cry.
> Men didn't come to see me, to let me cry and tell them how I
> felt. How was I to grieve over this loss? Men don't comfort each
> other during these painful times, but I am sure most men must
> have feelings similar to those I felt. Later, men told me they had
> seen me and turned away because they didn't know how to react
> or what to say.[2]

Coping with Expectations

A man usually reacts to loss based on the way (1) he was taught to
respond, (2) he is expected to respond, (3) he is predisposed to respond,
or (4) he is physically capable of responding.[3] Men follow the pattern of
what they observe, since no one ever teaches them explicitly. And they do
have to contend with cultural expectations, which is a source of additional pressure.

A man is expected to be in control, not lose it.

He's expected to be confident and assertive, not afraid, hesitant, anx-
ious, insecure, or sad.

He's supposed to be sufficient and know what he's doing, rational
and analytical, not passive, dependent, bewildered, or in need of support
or comfort.

Men are well aware of these expectations and try to live up to them.
They guard against what they must not be in the eyes of society.

Many factors create tension during a time of loss, however. Women
grow up with a rich vocabulary for their emotions, whereas men are raised
emotionally handicapped in their ability to express inner responses. And
when losses hit a family, they are compounded for the man, even though
he's unaware of it.

A man is supposed to be a competitor, but if his child dies, is disabled,
or rebels, he's defeated. He loses. He has failed in his role as a protector.
His grief impairs his functioning as a provider. He's supposed to be a problem solver, but he wasn't able to fix the problem with his child. He's no

longer in control of himself or the situation. Instead of being self- sufficient, he needs the assistance of others. His entire identity is threatened.[4]

Especially when his child dies, a father is also confronted with his own
mortality, the inevitability of his own death. *If something this bad can happen
to my child, none of us is safe.* For the father who has experienced little loss
in his life, it's even more difficult.

Further, when a child dies, other people usually look to the father as
the family protector or even the pillar of strength. They expect him to
take a leadership role. But as one father told me, "I don't want to be a
leader. Right now I want someone to take care of me, to minister to me.
Why should I receive any less than my wife and children?"

The two functions the father is expected to perform are making decisions and softening the blow for others. But why should that be? Both
the mother and father need to be involved in the decisions. If they're
not, resentment could build later if something did or didn't take place
counter to a wife's wishes. With Matthew, we were both involved in the
major decisions in his life, as well as following his death. We both felt
more support and comfort in that approach than we would have in trying to place it all on one person.

Attempting to cushion the blow for others is a form of denial that's
unhealthy for everyone. I've talked with fathers who wanted to tell others
they didn't feel they could cope anymore. But their resources were being
depleted guarding against that. I've talked with others who wanted to tell
people they were afraid, but they resisted it. I've talked with men who
told me they didn't "feel" during their loss. They just "handled it" and
moved ahead in life, unaware of the abundance of silent pain and hurt
screaming to be released. The cries were not heard.

Sometimes I'll keep pushing about the loss and how painful it must
have been, how empty the man must have felt, how much he must have
wanted to cry or become angry or yell. And in many cases, after ten to 15
minutes of encouraging the man to feel, the grief buried for years comes
rushing to the surface to be released. Often it's the first time someone
has encouraged him to grieve rather than reinforce his lack of grieving
with a comment like "You're doing so well. It's good to see you're strong
and relying on the Lord to keep you going." What a misperception of
strength and of God's expectations!

How Men Respond

How do men usually respond to their losses? With silence. Most men keep their feelings and thoughts bottled up. A quiet, introverted man is even more likely to react this way.

Listen to what several men said about their response:

> She got over the death of our daughter much faster than I did. I think it was because she spent so much time talking about it with her friends. I didn't feel like it was something I could talk to anybody about. I still don't. Women are much better with each other over things like that than men are. I didn't know how to handle it, and it was obvious that my friends didn't either. In fact, I think it made them uncomfortable just to be around me, knowing that I was upset. To be truthful, things haven't been the same between my friends and me ever since.

> The difference is that women talk their way through things and men think their way through things. Talking is something you do with somebody. Thinking is not. It stands to reason that

How do men usually respond to their losses? With silence.

women are going to spend more time with others when they have something important to deal with. Men, thinking alone, never really get at what is troubling them because they're not talking, not explaining, not asking questions, not using someone else to figure out their own feelings. Of course, they can't do that unless they are going to fully share all of what they are thinking. Men just don't do that with their friends.

> Women lighten their load by sharing the weight. We men tend to think it's the manly thing to do to carry all the weight our-

selves. That's why men get what I call "emotional hernias." We need to learn from women to share the load.[5]

A man's grieving pattern can make life more difficult for his wife and children, since they need him to talk and listen. They want to know about his heartache as well. Years ago, I used to wonder if I should bring up my feelings about a newly experienced loss that I felt over Matthew, but now I don't do any editing. I just come out with it, which helps both Joyce and me.

Few people ever asked how I was doing when they learned our son was mentally retarded. Fortunately, when Matthew died, people asked me as much as Joyce about my feelings. But too often the messages (including avoidance) a man receives verbally and nonverbally reinforce the expectation that "You're not going to get all emotional on me now, are you? You're not going to be vulnerable or afraid or cry or show me weakness, are you?" But why not? Why should we struggle to respond differently from the way God created us?

Perhaps the struggle is best depicted by this statement reflecting the pattern of our culture: "In our society men are taken seriously because they *don't* open up, because they *don't* talk about their feelings. Women aren't taken seriously because they *do* talk about their feelings."[6]

A second way men handle grief is by mourning alone or in secret. Men often give excuses for what they're doing or why they weren't at work rather than come out and say, "I was so overcome with grief over the loss that I wouldn't be able to function or help anyone at this time. I was hurting." Sometimes men grieve alone to not burden others, although they've been known to open up to strangers. And grieving alone fits many of the cultural expectations for the way men are "supposed" to behave. All this makes the emotions of grief a constant challenge to a man.

When you read the accounts of tragedies in the newspaper, the reports don't usually state that a woman was weeping. But they will say if a man was crying, since men aren't expected to do that. There's a message that crying should be confined to a funeral home or hospital, not done in public.

Sometimes in a hospital, if a person starts to cry in the corridor or waiting room, a nurse or doctor will say, "We have a room over here that you can use to cry in. You'll be more comfortable there." But perhaps it's not your comfort level they're concerned about but their own and that of others who are present. If a man cries in public, other people are usually very uncomfortable and want to stop him.[7]

Some men have never learned to cry outwardly. They cry only on the inside.

One of the most significant statements ever written on tears was by Max Lucado. As he put it, "When words are most empty, tears are most apt."[8]

After we learned the severity of our son's retardation, I didn't cry over it for months. I still had a sense of disbelief. One evening about ten months later, however, we were watching a television show called "Then Came Bronson" in which the main character traveled around the country on a motorcycle. In this particular episode, Bronson worked at a ranch for autistic children who couldn't speak. He worked with one child day after day and week after week. At the end of the program, the child spoke one word.

When I saw that, it was as if a key had unlocked the vault door holding back all my grief. As I felt the flood coming, I quickly left the room (the old message was intact—don't cry in front of anyone), went to the kitchen, and wept by myself. Fortunately, Joyce came in and held me so we could grieve together. We men need our turn to grieve, no matter what the loss.

William Schatz, a board member of the Compassionate Friends, told his story:

> Despite its perceived necessity, delay or postponement of grief can only last so long. The powerful emotional forces at work inside will eventually emerge in some fashion. They may come at a time when they are least expected, after it seems the worst is over. For me, it was 18 months after David died, and my wife was over her heavy grief work. Postponed grief seems to need some sort of catalyst to get things started. For me, it was a picture of David on our last vacation together, combined with the unconscious decision that the environment was safe enough to let the real feelings under the anger come to the surface. As I went by

that picture, I began to cry. Then I cried for 30 minutes. It seemed like I cried for all the times I had not cried since David had been diagnosed with leukemia—7 ½ years before. Each weekend for 4 weeks the same thing happened. It was a tremendous relief! I never thought that crying could feel so good. No one could have convinced me that it could relieve some of the hurt inside. One significant note: when I cried the first time, I was terrified that I would not be able to stop. Yet it felt so good that I soon forgot the scared feeling.[9]

Men do shed tears. We need to do it more frequently and more openly. Look at just one example in Scripture.

In Genesis 42—50, we find the account of Joseph's reunion with his brothers and father after years of separation. In his first contact with his brothers, Joseph said one of them would need to stay in Egypt. They became afraid of what might happen to them. As Joseph listened to them talking among themselves in his native language, his emotions surged to the surface, and "he turned away from them and began to weep" (Gen. 42:24).

Later, when his brothers returned to Egypt with their youngest brother, Scripture says, "Deeply moved at the sight of his brother, Joseph hurried out and looked for a place to weep." Eventually, he was so out of control that he "went into his private room and wept there" (Gen. 43:30). Notice the initial response of not crying in front of anyone. He wept uncontrollably again when his brother Judah made an offer to spare him from any more pain (see Gen. 45:2).

Joseph cried again when he revealed who he was to his brothers and father, as well as his plan to bring them all to Egypt to live with him. At that point, "he threw his arms around his brother Benjamin and wept, and Benjamin embraced him, weeping." Then "he kissed all his brothers and wept over them" (Gen. 45:14-15). Finally, he made his tears public and let others share them.

Three more times we have a record of Joseph's weeping: when his father arrived in Egypt, when his father died 17 years later, and when his brothers sent a message to him asking him to forgive them. The verse says, "When their message came to him, Joseph wept" (Gen. 50:17).[10]

When words fail, tears are the messenger. They are God's gift to all of us—men and women—to release our feelings. When Jesus arrived in Bethany following the death of Lazarus, He wept (see John 11:35). Ken Gire described the scene beautifully in *Incredible Moments with the Savior*.

When words fail, tears are the messenger.

On our way to Lazarus' tomb we stumble on still another question. Jesus approaches the gravesite with the full assurance that he will raise his friend from the dead. Why then does the sight of the tomb trouble him?

Maybe the tomb in the garden is too graphic a reminder of Eden gone to seed. Of Paradise lost. And of the cold, dark tomb he would have to enter to regain it.

In any case, it is remarkable that *our* plight could trouble *his* spirit; that *our* pain could summon *his* tears.

The raising of Lazarus is the most daring and dramatic of all the Savior's healings. He courageously went into a den where hostility raged against him to snatch a friend from the jaws of death.

It was an incredible moment.

It revealed that Jesus was who he said he was—the resurrection and the life. But it revealed something else.

The tears of God.

And who's to say which is more incredible—a man who raises the dead. . . or a God who weeps?[11]

Taking Action

Another way men deal with their grief is by taking either physical or legal action. This response is most often seen with the death of a child, but it's not uncommon when a child is disabled. There's a desire to fix blame and discover who else might be responsible. When a child is missing, usually the father is persistently action oriented, overcoming any obstacle in his way.

Part of this drive is the man's need to try to take back some control when a loss hits. Our culture expects it, and it's also one of our pillars of security. A loss wrestles control away from us, and in some way we want it back.

When a man confronts the feeling of helplessness by taking action, his anger becomes evident, for anger provides the energy that spurs the action. It's graphically seen in the grief responses of Vietnam veterans who lost friends or portions of their own bodies in the war.

When children are injured or killed, the rage over this tragedy and loss is best vented through constructive action. There is a down side to angry action, however. It can involve the man's thoughts and behavior so much that emotions such as sadness, despair, or longing have no opportunity to be felt and faced. Further, the anger's expression could become outwardly destructive or, if turned back upon himself, do internal damage. And it can keep him from responding to his wife's grief. He ends up grieving in solitude rather than with his spouse.

Activity is a response closely related to taking action. As a wife in counseling expressed it, "It's like he's on a treadmill. I wish he would sit still for a while. He just goes and goes and goes. And when I suggest that he cut back, he says it hurts too much when he does nothing." The husband's activity pattern can cause real problems in a family with a disabled child, because the wife has above-normal needs for support as she cares for their child.

When the news first hits a father about a serious problem with his child, work and household activity can help overcome the feelings of powerlessness and pain. The hours at work increase, or he gets overinvolved in fixing up the house. The pickup is noticeable to others for its intensity. If the man is already a workaholic or a type A personality, his activity level is often frenzied. The constant motion is like that of a hyperactive child who never runs down. And once again, the activity hinders dealing with his true feelings. It's a discomfort-blocking technique. Every man has a need to feel, whether he knows it or not. He needs to learn that feelings are a normal part of life.

Unfortunately, some of the activity may cross the boundary of healthy involvement and move into risk taking—things like driving fast, scuba diving, or drinking excessively.

A father described the way in which action played a part in his grief after his second child, an infant son, died 45 minutes after he was born:

"On the second day after losing Dax, I flew a newspaper assignment with the Air Force Reconnaissance unit through the eye of Hurricane Jeanne, some 400 miles out over the Gulf of Mexico, and I felt a lot better after rolling around in Death for a few hours. Being active— especially if there was some risk—compensated in a way for the horror of having to watch helplessly while a life I desperately wanted was snuffed out. If I kept busy, it would all go away. Or at least it wouldn't bother me. . . . But it did. There had been nothing I could do about it."[12]

A classic example of ongoing risk-taking behavior as a cover for grief is that of Houdini, the famous escape artist. His mother's death affected his actions to an extreme degree:

[He spent his life escaping from] straitjackets, all manner of manacles, chains, handcuffs, prison cells, chests, hampers, glass boxes, roll-top desks and even iron boilers. With his arms thoroughly secured he leaped from bridges; suspended head downward by block and tackle he loosened himself from meshes of constricting apparatus. He allowed himself to be chained and buried in six feet of earth, to be locked in steel vaults, to be nailed in huge packing cases. Once, breaking free after an endeavor lasting over an hour, he said: "The pain, torture, agony, and misery of that struggle will forever live in my mind." His variations on the escape act were endless, nothing being too bizarre, tedious, or difficult so long as the principles of a constraining force were present.[13]

Some pour their energy into recreational or sports activity, which in and of itself is not a problem. But it usually gets out of hand.[14]
Sometimes other people reinforce this problem by asking a father to take action. In the case of a stillbirth, for example, too often the hospital

staff expect the father to make the decisions about the disposition of the child's remains. He is advised to make the decision without involving the mother in order to spare her more trauma.

That practice is unfortunate, because it has numerous negative repercussions. In having to be the decision maker and action taker, the man has to suppress his grief. That keeps him from the positive experience of grieving and making decisions with his wife. And if he goes ahead and makes decisions on his own, his wife resents him for leaving her out of the process.[15]

When decisions need to be made for a disabled child's schooling or

*One other response to expect from a father: He'll do everything possible **not** to show his fear or insecurity.*

placement, or for removing the life-support systems from a brain-dead child, parents should make them jointly.

Some fathers exacerbate the difficulty by looking for solace and comfort apart from their marriages. Another woman who is not struggling with grief may be able to give more support. A new relationship with such a person may look inviting because the man sees it as relatively pain free. But it doesn't work. It simply postpones facing the grief.

We've seen many cases of divorced, bereaved fathers who had to face their grief years after they separated from their families. And when a disabled child is involved, there's great potential for a residue of guilt to accumulate if the family breaks up, because contact continues to some degree.

One other response to expect from a father: He'll do everything possible *not* to show his fear or insecurity. Men don't do well admitting to their fear. Years ago, I learned to ask my counselees (male and female), "What is the fear in your life that drives you?" Most of us are driven more by fear than drawn by hope. Our behavior certainly doesn't reflect fear, but often it could be prompted by fear.

A common male fear is, *If I show my despair or depression, how do I know that eventually I'll be okay? What's to keep it from going on and on?* Consider this message from a grief therapist to a man:

If you are among those who feel that you do not know how intense, lengthy, or deep your expression of grief may be, you may find yourself thinking that it would be impossible—or at least very difficult—for you to pull out of grief's deep pit to do all the things you need to do before or after the death. Being afraid of getting sucked down into a hollow of "no return" is not realistic. *Grief is not quicksand. Rather, it is a walk on rocky terrain that eventually smooths out and proves less challenging—both emotionally and physically.* So if you find yourself fearful of grieving, if you're imagining the worst or expecting some untenable transformation to take place within yourself, try putting those catastrophic thoughts in their proper perspective.

For example, you may think: *I will fall apart and won't be able to function if I start to show how I feel.* Replace such a thought with the more realistic: *I will let go for a time, release what I feel, and will be able to function better as a result of having vented the feelings that are an ever-present burden.*

You may think: *If I let myself grieve, then I will change permanently and won't ever be able to be myself again.* It's a fact that grief changes most survivors whether or not they vent their emotions and express their feelings. You can't keep change from happening after a loss; it is part of surviving a death. But you can take control over the type of change you experience. As you allow yourself to grieve, the changes that take place will be ones which allow you to go forward, to integrate loss, and to resolve the issues related to your loved one's death. Venting your responses can be like turning a searchlight on something moving in the shadows—which you imagine to be more enormous and menacing than it really is. Once the light is on, your caution seems to have been completely unnecessary.[16]

The Need for Full Expression

It's so much healthier for a man to go counter to society's expectations and feel and express his grief to the fullest. I know. I've been there. Fully grieving and expressing it show you're a man who accepts his maleness and humanity as created by God.

Perhaps the story of Cornelius can sum up a man's journey in grief and give us hope at the same time:

> Cornelius was a good looking, well-built black man in his late thirties. His dream was to be an Olympic gymnast, but Vietnam got in the way of his plans. A bullet not only injured his spinal cord and paralyzed his legs, but it also destroyed his dreams.
>
> Cornelius shared his healing process, which can be a message for all men:
>
> For the past three months I helped with a camp for disabled kids operated by the Crippled Children's Society. It's been twenty years since I lost the use of my legs, and I thought I was completely healed. However, during the first session of camp, I went through a grief process. At the end of the camping session, we had a time where all the counselors and campers told one another what they appreciated and learned from the whole week. Some were crying and grieving.
>
> I was crying, too. That's a sign of healing for me because I have not been able to cry in the past. Have you ever had a dream where you were falling and you can't stop yourself? That's the way I felt in that camp session. I knew more grief was working its way out. I knew I had to do something with my pain. I couldn't shut it down. I kept praying and asking God, "Who is going to help me?" God led a young man to me who was able-bodied, with a child-like innocence and acceptance. He was so fresh and so naive and nurturing. I talked to him and shared with him my fears, my anger and my hurt about all of these campers who were institutionalized in a society that doesn't seem to care about disabled people.
>
> "What will happen to all of these children?" I blurted out in

frustration. At that moment I recognized and acknowledged my own overwhelming fear that my children might become disabled. I broke down and grieved. I cried out loud like a baby. It was healthy. As I cried, this young man just held me. When I stopped, I had this tremendous peace. If I hadn't gone through that grieving process, I don't believe I would've been able to do the entire five sessions with those disabled kids. My friend let me fall into his arms when I was having the fear of falling into that pain and that pit. I knew I was getting better because this time I had the confidence that God would provide someone to hold me.

I have often wondered, *If I do open up, will anybody hold me? Will they be able to take what I let out?* When I was a child, I dreamed that I was falling, but I always woke up before I hit bottom. In real life we don't know if we're going to hit bottom or not. That fear is so overwhelming that we finally think, *Just let me hit the ground. Let me splatter.* As I let myself fall emotionally, the fear dissipated.

I now have a freedom that I never had before. I don't get headaches and jaw aches from trying to hold down the pain. I finally let that little child inside of me grieve. I didn't realize my fear was so great about my children. I was scared to death that my children would become disabled. I know I'm healing because I can admit my fears.[17]

When men experience a loss, let them grieve. Pay as much attention to them and care about them as much as you do the other family members. It will help!

⮜Ten⮞

What Do I Say to Others?

"I waited for days, even weeks before I could bring myself to tell anyone about our child," Susan said. "I used to think it wasn't because I was ashamed or embarrassed or anything, but I guess I did have those feelings. I don't know why I felt that way. Maybe I felt Jimmy's handicap was my fault, even though I knew it wasn't. It couldn't be. I guess I was afraid of their reaction. You never know what you're going to hear. I didn't want their advice. They're not experts, and I didn't want them telling me we were special parents and that's why God allowed us to have a child who will always be disabled."

Susan was experiencing the struggle of many parents: *Who can I tell about this, and what do I say?* This question is coupled with a fear of what you might hear from others. It's a legitimate concern, because people can make comments that cut you to the core. Sometimes their remarks that sound so definite are their way of hiding their anxiety about life's uncertainties. Or they simply don't know what to say. Most people don't intend to add to your pain or guilt, but an offhand comment can certainly do that.

Regardless of our fears, however, we all have some desire to tell others our troubles in order to gain comfort and support. And some people are indeed capable of helping us carry our burdens.

I remember talking with the father of a 16-year-old boy who had just been arrested for possessing drugs and driving under the influence. It was discovered that the boy had been using drugs for two years. The father was crying as he said, "My wife and I felt so isolated, so alone, and we didn't know what to do. But I was afraid to let others know. You know what I was afraid of? What would others think of us? I felt like such a failure, and I was sure they'd think we had failed. I could just hear them, 'Well, they really messed up as parents. Some moral teaching they gave him!' Maybe I was afraid of hearing statements I was saying about myself. I was afraid of being judged by other parents, because I felt like such a failure, like I did something wrong or this wouldn't have happened."

What a common dilemma! Whether your child takes a detour at age 12, 16, or 24, you struggle with your feelings about yourself and expect the wrath and judgment of others. And sometimes they are insensitive and judgmental. But most people are not; they're really fellow pilgrims walking the same boulder-strewn road.

You will find many people who have had similar experiences and are willing to help you work through this troubling time of life. I've taken the initiative many times in a counseling session or a seminar to describe the experiences we went through with Sheryl when she was 20 to 24. So often people are both surprised and relieved that someone else has been through what they're experiencing.

Sometimes when parents fumble with putting their concerns and feelings into words, I say, "Could it be you're struggling with how to tell others that your child is into drugs (alcohol, has AIDS, is living with someone, is gay, or is pregnant)? I understand your hesitation. It wasn't easy to tell others that our daughter had decided to live her life contrary to the Christian values she was raised with. It wasn't easy to say she was living with boyfriends, was using cocaine, and was becoming an alcoholic. Your dreams are shattered, and you ache inside.

"If anyone judged us, we never knew about it. I imagine some did. Some probably thought, *How can you teach on the family when your daughter is so fouled up?* I cannot control what others think and say. And as a parent, you always think about what you could have done differently. And yet often, you have done all you can to the best of your ability and dedicated that child to the Lord. There is that element of free will that you have no control over. God knows about that. He experienced it with the first two people He ever created. He understands and wants you to experience His comfort. I wonder what your struggle is?"

I have seen parents respond by breaking down and weeping, and part of the reason was the relief that someone else had been there and could understand and help. You'll find the support and comfort you need when you open your life to others.

Over the years, I've discovered that almost without exception, people who survive a personal or family crisis give credit to another family member or friend who supported them and gave them hope. When one crisis hits, we wonder when the next one will invade our lives. Left to ourselves, our fear mounts. But friends or trusted relatives have the ability to break the cycle of despair. They can help us see that we're not helpless and will find hope somewhere.

When you get the news about a serious problem with your child, however, you're overwhelmed. You may not have the opportunity to stabilize personally before you tell others. You probably share the news while you're still in turmoil. You want to tell people, and when you do, you're going to get some unedited reactions.

Three Common Reactions

You can anticipate at least three common reactions. One will be the inability of others to accept the bad news, especially news of a disability in another person. There are numerous reasons for this, but the results are the same. People can't handle the situation or accept the child. A similar response occurs when a child gets into difficulty.

No one should rob you of your feelings and your grief.

Often, others will verbalize sympathy and support, but their attitude and behavior may be rejecting. You end up wondering what's going on with the mixed messages. On the one hand, you feel them reaching out to you, but on the other, they're pulling away.

Remember that when other people are uncomfortable with your situation, they are feeling and, by their nonverbal responses, saying, "I want you 'normal' as soon as possible, or at least I want you to act that way." But you can't and won't be "normal" for some time, and no one else can determine how you should respond. This is your situation, your upset, your tragedy, and your loss. No one should rob you of your feelings and your grief. I read a statement once that describes death, but it applies to other situations as well: "When a person is born we celebrate; when they marry we jubilate; but when they die we act as if nothing has happened."[1]

Sometimes people's denial comes through with statements like "Your child will grow out of it," "The doctors don't know everything; they could be wrong, you know," or "Just say your child is slow or methodical and she'll catch up; don't give her the label 'retarded.'"

The more others hear about your difficulties, the greater the level of their discomfort, and they don't want your discomfort invading their lives. So they may distance themselves from you. I've seen situations where the parents, the children, or both were no longer invited to their friends' homes. You end up feeling they're afraid that what you've experienced may somehow be contagious.

It may help to explain some of the adjustments you're experiencing. If it was hard for you to accept the disability, say so. Tell people you understand how uncomfortable learning about this may be for them. Don't expect them to open up and say they're having difficulty with your situation. They probably won't. But if you admit your struggle with your mixture of feelings, at least they may feel more comfortable whether they admit anything or not.

Another problem you'll encounter is unsolicited advice. When you have a disabled child, you will receive it. When you have a child who strays, you'll get it. When you lose a child in death or a custody battle, you'll hear from others. Everyone is an expert or knows of a similar case, and since those who care about you want to help, they give emphatic suggestions about steps you should take. Sometimes they're offended if you don't show enthusiasm and indicate you're going to follow their advice immediately. Too often, however, their suggestions are contrary to your selected plan or the advice of your counselor or medical team.

Thank them for their concern and suggestions, and let them know they will add to the wealth of information you've been gathering. But if you're at a point where nothing is working, the experts don't know, or you're in a state of panic, you may jump from one piece of advice to another. Soon you'll be overwhelmed by a lack of follow-through on any of the suggestions. Before you take any suggestion, reflect on it. If you're still in a state of shock or crisis, let others help you make decisions.

In turning down the advice of others, you need to be firm and kind but not offensive. If you tend to be a dependent or submissive person, you'll struggle with how to respond. You may want to work out a statement to use with well-meaning people. You could say, "I appreciate your concern and suggestions the other day. We've decided to follow this plan at this time. We've considered the various options, and we're comfortable with this for the time being. If it doesn't work, we're open to other possibilities."

Sometimes it's not just advice you have to contend with, but also the third degree. You've probably heard the questions before. "Did anything happen during pregnancy? Has this happened before in your family? Was it the doctor's or hospital's fault? Do you have a good lawyer? Why did you allow him to go swimming there? Everyone knows how dangerous that place is!"

Yet another problem will be people who overwhelm you with help. For example, I've seen relatives and friends invade a family's boundaries and actually take away their decision-making opportunity. You need to determine how much assistance you want and establish boundaries with any intrusive friends or relatives. Most other people won't have any idea what you need or don't need until you outline it for them. They'll want to help, which is fine, but only you can determine the type and quantity of help you need.

A good starting point is to make a list of your needs and questions and then list the type of outside help you're looking for. It's all right to take the time to think, pray, and consider the options and the consequences of each. Don't let others pressure or rush you into anything.[2]

The Value of a Letter

One of the best ways I've discovered to explain your situation and your needs is to write and photocopy a letter you can give to relatives, friends, acquaintances, or anyone who asks. State what has happened, what it will be like for you, what they can expect from you, and what they can do for you.

By doing this, you ease some of your pain by not having to tell the same story over and over. (Sometimes the repetition intensifies the pain.)

Below are three separate letters you can use as models. The first reflects the loss of a child through death; the second, the discovery of a child's disability; and the last, a problem with a rebellious child.

Dear Friend, (or family, fellow workers, etc.),

Just recently I have suffered a major loss in my life, the death of my daughter. My wife and I are grieving and it's going to take months and even years to recover from this loss. We are still shocked by what happened.

I wanted to let you know that I will cry from time to time. I can't tell you what will set me off and I don't apologize for my tears since they are not a sign of weakness or a lack of faith. They are God's gift to me to express my protest and feelings of sadness over the loss and they help me recover.

At times you may see me angry for no apparent reason. Sometimes I'm not even sure why, but it happens. All I know is that all my emotions are intense because of my grief. If I don't always make sense to you or stop in the middle of a sentence, please be patient with me. I'm not going crazy and if I repeat myself again and again, please accept this as normal.

I guess I need your presence and your understanding and your care more than anything. You don't always have to know what to say or even say anything if you don't know how to respond. Just being there or a touch or a hug lets me know you care. Please don't wait for me to call or reach out since sometimes I'm too tired or despondent to do so.

If I tend to withdraw or cut myself off from you, please don't let me do that. I need you to reach out to me for months and even years.

I'd like you to pray for me that I will come to see some meaning or purpose in all this. Right now I don't and can't and anything that anyone says right now does not help. You can pray that I would know God's comfort and love.

If you've ever experienced a similar type of loss, please feel free to share it with me. It will help me rather than make me feel worse. And don't stop sharing if I choke up or start to cry. It's all right and I won't be bothered if you end up crying too.

This loss is so painful and right now feels like the worst thing that could ever happen to me. But I will survive and recover. At times I don't feel that way, but I know it will happen. I hold on to that hope. I know that I won't always feel as I do now.

Thank you for caring about me, for listening and for praying. Your concern comforts me and is a gift for which I will always be thankful.[3]

Touch carries a healing quality.

Touch carries a healing quality. Don't hesitate to ask for a hug from someone close to you when you need it. One person who experienced a loss put it this way:

> Your mind is still on crutches. . . . There is something awe-inspiring, silencing and shattering about emotional pain that does leave one at a loss for words. Perhaps gestures are better. I've mentioned before my need for hugs. I'm sure other people feel the same way. Human physical comfort, no strings, I saw a cartoon once, no caption. . . . It was a vending machine, the sign on it read, "Hugs 25 cents." I wish I could have one installed.[4]

One day I received a special gift in this way. As a counselor, I'm called to give care to those who come to me for help. It's a role I accept from the Lord as a ministry. But occasionally, the roles are dramatically reversed, as they were in my office that day.

Rick came in to talk about some problems he was having. In the course of our conversation, he noticed the latest photograph of our family I had on display. He asked about them, and I mentioned that Matthew was now with the Lord. Rick asked a number of questions about Matthew and discovered how limited his abilities had been. Then he said, "I guess you never experienced what most fathers experience with their sons, did you, Norm? You never played ball with Matthew, never took him fishing, and never heard him tell you what most sons say to their dads growing up. And you only experienced a few hugs from him, right?"

I nodded silently as tears began to fill my eyes at the sensitive words and fresh thoughts of Matthew.

Rick continued, "Well, just remember, Norm. When you die and arrive in heaven, your Matthew will come running up to you and, with his newfound abilities, throw his arms around your neck and say, 'Daddy, I love you.'"

By then my tears were flowing freely. I said, "Thank you for saying that, Rick. No one has ever told me that before."

Rick smiled, got up, came over, and gave me a big hug. A new bond was established between us that day as I realized again that counselees can also minister to counselors.

The second letter is from the parent of a disabled child:

Dear Friend (family member, fellow worker),

Just recently I was told that our child is profoundly retarded and will always be like this. I guess I'm still in a state of both shock and grief. I'm not even sure where to go from here. So if I'm not the way I usually am, there's a good reason for it, and I wanted you to be aware of it. There will be times when I'm depressed or angry or I'll cry during the middle of a conversation. I can't always tell you why I'm responding that way. Just let me express what I'm feeling. Please don't take it personally or try to fix me. If I don't always make sense to you or repeat myself, just accept this as normal.

Part of my struggle is accepting the fact that my son is retarded. There are times when I blame God or anyone else who gets in the way. I wish I wasn't the parent of a child like this. At times I feel like I don't even want him. Yet I know I love him. But all I see in the future is always being the parent of a retarded child, with no change or no hope of anything different.

There may be times when you have mixed feelings, too. You may not be comfortable around our son since he may continue to drool, his coordination won't be good, and eventually, he won't look like other kids. I can understand your hesitation. It's all right if you can't handle being around our son. I hope you will be able to be around us, since we need your understanding and your presence. When you ask how I'm doing, I'll be honest and tell you. There will be times when I'll let you know what I need, and maybe between us we can figure out what to do.

If you give me advice or suggestions, I will consider them. Perhaps at times I'll follow them, and at times I'll follow the plan or course we're already on.

Above all, I need your prayer support. I need God's comfort and love. If you know of others who have traveled this same path, let me know who they are, since they may be able to help me.

Thank you for your care and support and listening ear. Your support means much to me.

Here's the letter from the parent of a rebellious child:

Dear Friend (or whomever),

You may have heard that we've had some difficulty with our oldest daughter. This has been very hard for my husband and me, and sometimes we're embarrassed over what has happened. Who would have expected that she would use drugs, leave high school, and live on the streets! The reason for this letter is that it's too painful to have to explain this over and over to our friends and relatives. We wish the problem would go away or that we could just hide. But it doesn't and we can't, and we don't have any idea how this is going to turn out or when it will be over.

Please just keep asking us how we're doing and continue to pray for us. We probably won't be the same each time you talk with us. We could be angry one time or depressed and dejected another. Help us to talk, and just listen. If you have some suggestions, we will consider them, and perhaps something you say will benefit us.

You may find yourself with many questions as well as feelings, too. You may be shocked and find yourself angry, wishing you could talk to our daughter and knock some sense into her head. You may even wonder, as we did, where we went wrong. What could we have done differently so this would not have happened? If you hear anyone judging us, please let them know we are already doing this and need their understanding.

Please don't withdraw from us. We need your support more than ever. Pray for us as well as our daughter. We want to continue to love her, encourage her, and believe in her. Pray that we won't just concentrate on our hurt but on her needs as well. Don't be surprised if we call you from time to time and say we need to talk, or ask you to go to dinner and talk about everything other than our daughter, since we need a break.

This is a loss to us and to our other children, and it's painful. Thank you for your support.

When you take a positive, assertive step in reaching out to others and letting them know what you need, you'll gain confidence and strength. You'll feel less like a victim. Above all, talk about your feelings and concerns with family members. Don't try to protect them from the news, no matter what the problem, and be aware of the danger of neglecting them because of all the attention given to the problem.

No matter what you say, your nonverbal communication and tone of voice will convey a stronger message. If you have other children, what you tell them needs to be appropriate to their age and developmental levels. As your situation changes, you'll need to update them.

If a child has died, in addition to experiencing your own grief, you may need to assist your children in grieving properly. If one of your children is rebelling, you may be struggling with the problem of not letting that child become a role model for younger siblings. You may need the help of a counselor in knowing exactly what to say and do.

When you have a disabled child, it may be more difficult for others to understand, especially if the child looks "normal." Dr. Rosemarie Cook described the stress you'll experience when you raise a disabled child:

Any of several possible events can cause you stress. Your disabled child could be in a life-threatening situation. The child could be medically stable but require intense care at home. You may be frustrated with not knowing what is wrong and may be searching for help and resources. Any of these situations can drain your limited emotional energy, time, and finances. You have only so much to give out in a twenty-four hour day. You need a certain amount of rest and nourishment. Your mind needs time to process and sort. Your bank accounts have clear limits.

When your family has a child with a disability, it's almost as if you are on an amusement park ride. When you step into the car of a roller coaster, someone else holds the controls. There are no stops or stations along the way. You are committed to be in that car until the end of the ride. The care of your child will be a constant in your life; you're on the ride until it stops. You won't have the luxury of stopping the ride for a rest. You will have family business, other children, and other stresses to cope with in addition to the child with special needs.

Modeling provides a powerful learning experience. Your children will do as you do, not as you say. If there is a discrepancy between your words and your actions, your children will choose to imitate your actions. Actions result from attitudes, so in imitating parental actions, children incorporate parental attitudes without conscious awareness. The messages, then, that you send to your other children are the messages that you tell yourself and each other.[5]

As you consider sharing your situation with others, the One to take it to daily is the One who can provide the comfort and strength you need. Sometimes, because of feeling overwhelmed, you may tend to put distance between yourself and God. Or you could be angry with Him. In either case, don't withdraw. Reach out. Tell Him all your feelings. You may want to begin a daily journal to help in clarifying your feelings and progress.

Perhaps the best thing to tell others can be summed up in this phrase: "The truth; nothing but the truth."

ᴇElevenᴇMed

Why Me?

YOU won't be the last person to ask God, "Why?" And believe me, you're not the first. Many years ago, one of His prophets asked the same question, and he wasn't indirect or timid, either. He was appalled by all the suffering he saw, just as some of us are today. This is what he said to God:

> How long, O LORD, will I call for help, and Thou wilt not hear? I cry out to Thee, "Violence!" Yet Thou dost not save. Why dost Thou make me see iniquity, and cause me to look on wickedness? Yes, destruction and violence are before me; Strife exists and contention arises. Therefore, the law is ignored and justice is never upheld. For the wicked surround the righteous; Therefore, justice comes out perverted. (Hab. 1:2-4, NASB)

When we encounter the deep valleys in our lives, they soon reflect our theology and philosophy of life. Unfortunately, our expectations and beliefs sometimes don't correspond to Scripture. But that doesn't mean we're heretics. Rather, through the trying times, we have the opportunity to bring our thinking and perspective into line with God's Word. When a child dies, is disabled, or wanders, some of our beliefs are challenged.

Many Christians believe, for example, that life is (or ought to be) fair. They think, *If I'm a Christian, I'm immune to tragedy.* God does not insulate us from misfortunes, however, and He never promised He would. Sometimes God does intervene in a strange and marvelous way, but it's at His sovereign choosing and not through our demanding.

You may have difficulty understanding the interplay between God's sovereignty and our free will. Most of us do. No one likes suffering or tragedy, especially when it happens to a child. What happens to our kids will change our lives forever, especially our perspective of and relationship with God.

A couple who live not far from us have not just one but two mentally retarded children. They've been through intense struggles. But they stand as a witness that in spite of the turmoil, a marriage with Jesus Christ at the center can not only survive but even blossom. Theirs came back from the precipice of disaster. In a book about their son, Craig, Gloria Hawley tells their story. This incident reflects the emotional upheaval in their time of despair:

> Shortly before Craig's fifth birthday, a skull X-ray revealed a walnut-sized mass in his brain. The surgery would be extensive and risky.
>
> The capricious fist of God seemed to descend on the family once more, smashing peace and laughter and hope. Chan and Gloria felt helpless in their pitiful attempts to love and protect their children! God was NOT "love"—if so, how could He continually inflict pain on innocent children and threaten their beloved son with paralysis or death?
>
> "I hate You, God!" snarled Gloria in her fury. "You leave my children ALONE!" She had learned during Laura's infancy that it did not pay to plead or bargain with God. And as for His Son—that remote and cardboard wimp—she had no need for Him either.
>
> The Hawleys knew about Jesus—as much as they cared to know. Gloria privately kept Him in a dim corner of her mind, enclosed in a case labeled, "Break glass in case of emergency." In that split second before death, she would "break the glass" by saying "Okay, I believe in You, Jesus"—thus insuring a heavenly eternity. Until that time, she railed against the plight of her babies and squandered her energies in vain attempts to make them "well." Gloria had a secret dread, never voiced, that drove her to greater and greater efforts to establish Laura and Craig within

the charmed circle of normality: a horror of seeing those lovely, appealing little ones grow to grotesque maturity as adult retardates. As a nurse, Gloria knew that every flaw in the children could become magnified and distorted in later years. She had seen people like that.

HER children would not become repugnant, objects of ridicule and rejection. Laura and Craig were not to suffer such a fate if she had to move heaven and hell to accomplish that goal!

Gloria's obsession with her children, her constant anxiety, hostility, and fear slowly poisoned her personality and emotional health. She fought with doctors, therapists, nurses, teachers, principals, technicians, psychologists—everybody in the "System." Some of the battles were justified, but much more could have been accomplished without her ever-present rage.

Her rage was actually directed against God. She had no difficulty with the theological principle of the sovereignty of God; she *knew* that the affliction of her beloved little ones was *all His fault!*[1]

But then, through the prayers of people all over the country, the mass disappeared. Even the neurosurgeon was baffled. Their son was alive and could go home:

Alive. Gloria wished she could say the same for herself. The incredible pressure of the crisis and the daily routine with two multihandicapped children was more than she could bear.

Within months of Craig's surgery Gloria found herself at the end of her hope, health, strength—and marriage. As she lay in a hospital bed, hemorrhaging from colitis, she weakly sought the Lord whom she had so long despised. In her innermost being, she had refused the ancient Love that the soul recognizes instinctively. "Oh, please forgive me, and live my life *because I can't!*" she desperately implored. "Please, Jesus, hear me! I can't go on . . . come into my heart and live my life! It's over without You."

He heard. He came. He began to heal her from within. And He never, never left her.

When Gloria went home from the hospital, she was faced with the consequences of her willful ways—but she did not face them alone![2]

I've talked to some people who have said, "Of course God doesn't understand the extent of my pain. If He did, and if He loves us as He says, He would put an end to it. I wish He cared more." But He does care—more than we know. He's been where we are. In *Helping People Through Grief*, Delores Kuenning explains:

We all fear pain; yet from infancy it serves as a warning mechanism within our bodies to protect us from the hot stove or alert us to an inflammatory process within. But when it ravages our bodies, or the body of a loved one, it sears the soul and torments us physically, emotionally, and spiritually. *Why does God allow suffering?* we ask. *Does suffering have meaning?*

Daniel Simundson, in *Where Is God in My Suffering?* reminds us that "when we cry out to God in our times of suffering, we know that we will be heard by One who truly knows what we have gone through. It is a great comfort for a sufferer to know the presence of an understanding and compassionate God, who not only invites our very human prayers but also knows what it is like to be in so much pain. God hears. God understands. God suffers with us. The lament is heard by One who has been there."[3]

His Son was brutally murdered. He does understand. Read His story; it's there in the Gospels.

If God Is All-Powerful . . .

The source for what we believe has to be the Word of God. And it states time and again that God is good and has a concern for humanity. We also know He is omnipotent. That means He's all-powerful. But what does *all-powerful* mean to you? Sometimes we attribute incorrect meanings to it. Does it mean we're robots and that He causes every single thing that happens in the world?

God's omnipotence does *not* necessarily mean that everything happens the way He wants it. At the dawn of the world, He created human beings with the ability to make choices. Because of our choices, things

God could not give us the freedom to love Him if we didn't have the freedom to reject Him and His teachings.

happen that are not what He desires. God could not give us the freedom to love Him if we didn't have the freedom to reject Him and His teachings. He wants us to love Him based on our choice.

Dr. Dwight Carlson, a friend and Christian psychiatrist, has seen his adult daughter battle leukemia. He gave her his bone marrow as a transplant. In his book *When Life Isn't Fair,* he wrote,

> It is further possible that since God greatly desires individuals who willingly love, worship, and follow Him, He had no alternative but to allow Satan to test them with pain, suffering, and misfortune. This is one of the major points taught in the Book of Job. Let me assure you that this does NOT mean God is not sovereign; in the Book of Job, Satan had to request permission to test Job, and God allowed it only within very fixed limits (Job 2:6).
>
> Recognition of God's self-imposed limitations is the most difficult concept to grasp in this book. Many ardent Christians will have difficulty with this view point. But I am convinced that when God created the world, He set laws in motion which even He chooses to honor. The problem for us is that these laws intersect our lives in the most sensitive areas—in our suffering and misfortune.[4]

When the suffering hits our children, we plead with Him. And when our request seems to fall on deaf ears, we tell God that something is wrong with Him and the way He's running the world. It sure seems that way. Most of us usually put faith in formulas. We feel comfortable with predictability, regularity, and assurance. Don't you? We want God to be that way as well, so we try to create Him in the image of what we want Him to be and do.

None of us can predict what God will do, however. Paul reminded us of that in Romans 11:33: "O the depth of the riches both of the wisdom and knowledge of God! How unsearchable are his judgments, and his ways past finding out!" (KJV).

God is not uncaring or busy elsewhere. He is neither insensitive nor punitive. He is supreme, sovereign, loving, and sensitive.

I don't fully comprehend God. I, too, have unanswered questions about some of the events of my life. But all our trials, problems, crises, and suffering occur by divine permission. As Don Baker put it:

> God allows us to suffer. This may be the only solution to the problem that we will ever receive. Nothing can touch the Christian without having first received the permission of God. If I do not accept that statement, then I really do not believe that God is sovereign—and if I do not believe in His sovereignty, then I am helpless before all the forces of heaven and hell.[5]

God allows suffering for His reasons. We can fight and argue against this truth, or we can learn to see God as the gracious controller of the universe. He is free to do as He desires, and He doesn't have to give us explanations. People in our independent-minded culture can't seem to fathom that. We feel God owes us an accounting. But He doesn't. He has already given us His Son and His Holy Spirit to strengthen and guide us. We look at problems and losses and say, "Why?" Jesus asks us to look at them and say, "Why not?"

Growing Through the Pain

God allows us to experience things for our growth. He has arranged the seasons of nature to produce growth, and He arranges the seasons of our lives for growth as well. Some days bring sunshine, and some bring storms. Both are necessary. He knows the amount of pressure we can handle. First Corinthians 10:13 declares that He will "not let you be tempted beyond what you can bear." But He does let us be tempted, feel pain, and experience suffering.

As we cared for our disabled child, we learned and grew. We had to in order to survive. We learned the meaning of Matthew's name, which is "God's gift" or "gift of God." We learned that with the difficulties of life, God either gives you the resources to handle them at that time, or He

> *We learned to stop depending on our own resources so much and to rely on God and His grace.*

has prepared you in advance, even though you may not be aware of it. That's what He did in our case. Why? We don't know. We're just so thankful He did. And the way God reaches out to strengthen us is unique for every person. We learned to stop depending on our own resources so much and to rely on God and His grace.

God gives us the grace to live whether the sun is shining or we feel as if we're being tossed around by a savage tornado. Grace is really God's assurance that life can be all right when everything in it is all wrong. It's the power to live today as if things will be all right tomorrow. Lewis Smedes described it graphically:

> Grace does not make everything right. Grace's trick is to show us that it is right for us to live; that it is truly good, wonderful even, for us to be breathing and feeling at the same time that everything clustering around us is wholly wretched. Grace is not a ticket to Fantasy Island; Fantasy Island is dreamy fiction. Grace is not a potion to charm life to our liking; charms are magic. Grace does not cure all our concerns, transform all our kids into winners, or send us all soaring into the high skies of sex and success. Grace is rather an amazing power to look earthy reality full in the face, see its sad and tragic edges, feel its cruel cuts, join in the primeval chorus against its outrageous unfairness, and yet feel in your deepest being that it is good and right for you to be alive on God's good earth.[6]

We learned the truth and significance of many passages from God's Word. Over the years, one passage in particular came alive as we depended on it more and more: "Consider it all joy, my brethren, when you encounter various trials, knowing that the testing [or trying] of your faith produces endurance" (James 1:2-3, NASB). The Amplified version says, "But let endurance and steadfastness and patience have full play and do a thorough work, so that you may be [people] perfectly and fully developed (with no defects), lacking in nothing" (James 1:4).

Learning to put that into practice is a process. And the passage does not say "respond this way immediately." You have to feel the pain and grief first, and then you'll be able to consider it all joy.

What does the word *consider* mean? As I studied in commentaries, I discovered that it refers to an internal attitude of the heart or mind that allows the trials and circumstances of life to affect us adversely or beneficially. Another way James 1:2 might be translated is this: "Make up your mind to regard adversity as something to welcome or be glad about."

You have the power to decide what your attitude will be. You can say about a trial, "That's terrible. Totally upsetting. That's the last thing I wanted for my life. Why did it have to happen now? Why me?"

The other way of "considering" the same difficulty, however, is to say, "It's not what I wanted or expected, but it's here. There are going to be some difficult times, but how can I make the best of them?" Don't ever deny the pain or hurt you might have to go through, but always ask, "What can I learn from it? How can I grow through this? How can I use it for God's glory?"

The verb tense used in the word *consider* indicates a decisiveness of action. It's not an attitude of resignation—"Well, I'll just give up. I'm stuck with this problem. That's the way life is." If you resign yourself, you will sit back and not do anything. But James 1:2 indicates you will have to go against your natural inclination to see the trial as a negative. There will be some moments when you'll have to remind yourself, "I think there's a better way of responding to this. Lord, I really want You to help me see it from a different perspective." Then your mind will shift to a more constructive response. But this often takes a lot of work on your part.

God created us with both the capacity and the freedom to determine how we respond to the unexpected incidents life brings our way. You may wish that a certain event had never occurred, but you can't change the facts.

One of the best ways to clarify our response to what we can't understand, explain, or like is set forth in a phrase by Dr. Gerald Mann. He suggests that we are "free to determine what happens to what happens to us."[7] Did you catch that? It's a choice.

Viktor Frankl, a Jewish physician sent to a death camp by the Nazis, learned this same truth. One day at the prison, an exceptionally cruel guard saw that Frankl still had his wedding band and took it from him. It was Frankl's last possession that gave him a link to the past, for his parents, wife, and children had been killed in the gas chamber. And all his papers and photos had been taken from him.[8] The story continues:

> As he stood looking into the mocking face of the guard, a totally unexpected thought flooded his consciousness. He realized that there was one thing, and only one thing, that the guard could not take from him: namely, *how he chose to feel* about the guard and what the guard was doing to him.
>
> "Everything can be taken from a man but one thing," said Frankl, "the last of human freedoms—to choose one's attitude in any given set of circumstances."[9]

Isn't that what Paul was saying in Philippians 4:12? "I know how to be abased and live humbly in straitened circumstances, and I know also how to enjoy plenty and live in abundance. I have learned in any and all circumstances, the secret of facing every situation, whether well-fed or going hungry, having a sufficiency and to spare or going without and being in want" (AMPLIFIED). And his contentment came from the strength Christ gave him (see Phil. 4:13).

You and I have a choice—not about the difficulties of life, for they're inevitable, but about joy, for it's always an option!

John Killinger offers this helpful perspective on how we handle life's difficulties:

> Somehow, joy arises from loss and suffering and toil as much as it does from pleasure and ease. It is much deeper than the sur-

face of existence; it has to do with the whole structure of life. It is the perfume of the rose that is crushed, the flash of color in the bird that is hit, the lump in the throat of the man who sees and knows, instinctively, that life is a many splendored thing.

Don't misunderstand me. I am not suggesting that God sends adversity to enhance our appreciation of life or to make us more aware of His nearness. Nor am I implying that the fullness of life comes only to those who have passed through deep waters. Rather, I am saying that God is present in all of life, including its tragedies. His presence transforms even these agonizing experiences into opportunities for worship.[10]

During the time of anguish as well as all the other times of life, our stability comes from our Lord. God's Word says, "Now to Him who is able to establish you according to my gospel and the preaching of Jesus Christ, according to the revelation of the mystery which has been kept secret for long ages past" (Rom. 16:25, NASB).

"Then he said to them, 'Go, eat of the fat, drink of the sweet, and send portions to him who has nothing prepared; for this day is holy to our Lord. Do not be grieved, for the joy of the LORD is your strength'" (Neh. 8:10, NASB).

"And He shall be the stability of your times, a wealth of salvation, wisdom, and knowledge; the fear of the LORD is his treasure" (Isa. 33:6, NASB).

God is the ultimate resource.

> *During the time of anguish as well as all the other times of life, our stability comes from our Lord.*

This is the message of Job: "Though he [God] slay me, yet will I trust in him" (Job 13:15, KJV).

This is the message of David: "Yea, though I walk through the valley of the shadow of death, I will fear no evil: for thou art with me; thy rod and thy staff they comfort me" (Ps. 23:4, KJV).

This is the message of Isaiah: "Thou wilt keep him in perfect peace, whose mind is stayed on thee: because he trusteth in thee" (Isa. 26:3, KJV).

This is the message of Paul: "For I am persuaded, that neither death, nor life, nor angels, nor principalities, nor powers, nor things present, nor things to come, nor height, nor depth, nor any other creature, shall be able to separate us from the love of God, which is in Christ Jesus our Lord" (Rom. 8:38-39, KJV).

Where Are You?

Where are you in terms of the questions you're asking? Are you able to say:

What can I learn from this?

How can I grow through this?

How can God be glorified through this?

The time will come when you'll be able to ask these questions, and they will be answered.[11]

Remember the question asked by the prophet Habakkuk at the beginning of this chapter? Although his *why* seemed to go unanswered, he eventually came to the place of confidence and hope:

> Though the fig tree should not blossom, and there be no fruit on the vines, though the yield of the olive should fail, and the fields produce no food, though the flock should be cut off from the fold, and there be no cattle in the stalls, yet I will exult in the LORD, I will rejoice in the God of my salvation. (Hab. 3:17-18, NASB)

The word *rejoice* means "to leap for joy and spin about in exultation." That isn't happiness, which depends on having no problems or concerns. Rather, joy is having faith in God regardless of circumstances.

Over the years, we have learned from and been ministered to by the struggles and insights of others. Sometimes we've learned from watching them, talking to them, or reading what they've written. There will be times when you're involved in learning, but you need someone else to come along and summarize it for you. Recently, I came across such a statement that opened my eyes once again. Perhaps it did so because I've raised a disabled child, I'm 55 years old at the time of this writing, and I'm helping to care for our elderly mothers (ages 88 and 92).

R. Scott Sullender, a pastor, wrote these penetrating words:

There is a handicapped person in your future: you! Handicapped persons are dealing in the present moment with what you and I will have to deal with later. Sooner or later each of us will become handicapped in one way or another. Sooner or later each of us will have to deal with one or several major losses in our health. Then we will travel down the same path that the handicapped person currently walks. Then we will know their pain, frustration and sufferings. Perhaps if we could learn from them now, whatever our age, we would be better prepared for our own future.

Handicapped persons teach us that life is more than a body. They demonstrate the truth of all of the great religions that the things that make us truly human and truly divine are not physical qualities. They are qualities of the Spirit. St. Paul listed a few of these qualities: love, joy, peace, patience, kindness, goodness, faithfulness, gentleness, self-control (Gal 5:22). Jesus listed a few more: meekness, peacemaking, purity of heart, mercy, hunger for righteousness, suffering in a right cause (Mt 5:3-10). Neither of them mentioned physical beauty or even physical health. The qualities that save us do not include the shape of our bodies.

Handicapped persons also can teach us how to suffer and how to rise above bodily limitations. Sometimes pain cannot be fixed, nor can all limitations be conquered. Most of us will have to deal with pain and limitations, at first in minor ways and later in major ways. We will learn new meanings for the word "courage." Either we will rise above our limitations and learn to live with them or we shall sink to new lows of despair, bitterness and helplessness. The choice depends largely on the strength of our courage.

In a sense, then, a handicap or a loss of health can become a gift. It never starts out that way. Initially it is a horrible loss. If through the loss, however, we can learn to nurture our spiritual qualities and learn the art of suffering well, then we will have transformed our loss into a gain. We will have grown in and through our loss. We will have risen above our loss precisely by not letting it defeat us, but by letting it propel us forward into a more advanced stage of human existence. Admittedly, not everyone makes such a major leap forward. Neither have some human beings made it past a Sunday school theology. Yet, the loss of health in later life, as horrible as it seems, can be the opportunity for growing toward an even greater level of spiritual maturity.[12]

As we were recovering from Matthew's death, the times of sorrow grew further and further apart. Unfortunately, the sharpness of human memories tends to fade as time goes on. And that's something we resist, since that is all we have. But often, when you least expect something new to come into your life to affect you, it happens. It did to us on August 15, 1991—the day Matthew would have observed his twenty-fourth birthday.

God's Grace

Any anniversary is painful when the loss is fresh. But that evening, we contacted an attendant who had cared for Matthew at Salem Christian Home, his residence for the last 11 years of his life. A friend said the woman wanted to tell us some of her experiences with Matthew.

As we talked over the phone, she told us about several aspects of Matthew's life we had never seen. She described how he had learned to put together a very simple puzzle. When she took him for a walk outside, Matthew would walk way ahead and then try to hide from her. She described how he had learned to dry his hair with a dryer, and how he would turn it around and blow it on her hair.

One day she took her six-month-old baby to the dorm for all the residents to see. She placed her baby in Matthew's arms and reached around him to help hold her little girl. As she did, she rocked them a bit as she sang "Rock a Bye Baby," and she noticed tears running down our son's face. We were amazed at the news. The woman had given us a wonderful memory.

To someone who has never raised a disabled child, those events might not seem like much. But because Matthew's limitations were so massive and the ordinary experiences of life were so few, knowing those additional experiences of our son was an immeasurable blessing for us.

I never cease to marvel at God's timing. The very next day, I received a letter from a woman who had written me some time earlier. Her first letter described how a healing had taken place between her and her 83-year-old father. A quarter-century rift between them had been mended, and a new bonding had occurred. She wanted to tell me because my book *Always Daddy's Girl* had helped her with this relationship. She also asked if I would pray for her father, who hadn't yet trusted in Jesus Christ as his personal Savior.

In the new letter, the woman said her father had finally become a Christian the year before. She went on to say that he had died just three months later, and she enclosed a written portrayal of her last visit with him. I reprint it here, with her permission, because it provides a beautiful picture of the passages of life through which we all move, and it describes how all of us will ultimately be disabled until Jesus reaches out and calls us home:

Midlife. A reversal of roles. Dad is the child now and I am the parent.

We got word that his heart was failing. He had made a valiant effort to come to his granddaughter's wedding, but the trip proved to be too much for him. Upon arrival at the wedding, he looked ashen gray. Everyone was concerned about him. I reassured myself that with a little rest next week, he would be fine. But next week came, and along with it the alarming news. He was listless, unable to be aroused at times, pale and trembling, and his legs and ankles were very swollen. All symptoms of congestive heart failure. He needed to be seen by a doctor.

As a daughter, my heart was heavy with the thought of losing Dad. Tears flowed freely as I prayed for another opportunity to be with him before he died. How I longed to tell him one more time how much he meant to me. You see, our relationship now as father and daughter was a very simple, yet tender one. Each time I visited him, I would remind him that he gave out hugs like no one else could, and that I still needed him to be my Dad. His face always beamed when he was reminded.

When packing my bags to make the four-hour journey to his home, thoughts turned to a book that I had recently given to my daughters. It was a children's book that told how love is passed from one generation to another. I tucked it into my suitcase, hoping to be able to share it with Dad.

Upon arriving, the doctor confirmed our suspicion—it was congestive heart failure. Dad could have another heart attack at any moment. The doctor requested that I stay with him for the next week to monitor his condition.

The second evening after dinner, I told Dad that I wanted to share something with him—a story about him and me. He responded appreciatively to my request to read the story to him. As I began to read, emotion engulfed my voice. The story began with the child as a baby being rocked in the arms of the parent, and having this song sung to him:

"I'll love you forever,
I'll like you for always,
As long as I'm living
my baby you'll be."

As the story unfolded of the child passing through the various stages of childhood into maturity, Dad listened with enjoyment. At every stage of development, the parent would sing the same verse to the child. He looked at the pictures with childlike eagerness, commenting on them every now and then. At that moment came the realization that the roles had been reversed. I was now the parent, reading a story to the child. It felt strange. But it was all right, for that's the way that life is sometimes. Roles do change as we pass from one stage of life into another.

In the story, years after the child had reached maturity the parent became elderly and frail. The picture showed a frowning man holding his dying mother in his arms, rocking her and singing this song:

"I'll love you forever,
I'll like you for always,
As long as I'm living
my Mommy you'll be."

"That's how I feel about you, Dad. I will love you forever!"
Tears filled both our eyes, and he hugged me once again.

The days of our visit quickly passed, and it was time to make
the four-hour return trip home. My family was expecting me for
dinner that evening. It would be difficult to leave Dad, knowing
that I may never see him again this side of heaven. But the Lord
had already assured me that someday in heaven, we will be
reunited. Now my calling as a parent will be to go back home to
the next generation and pass on the song that Dad has sung to
me in every stage of life:

"I'll love you forever,
I'll like you for always,
As long as I'm living
my baby you'll be."[13]

May God bless you in your journey through life, and may you experience His grace during its joys and sorrows.

Additional Resources

Printed Materials

Martha Jo Church, Helene Chazin, and Faith Ewald. *When a Baby Dies.* Available from the Compassionate Friends, P.O. Box 3696, Oak Brook, IL 60522-3696.

Glen W. Davidson, M.D. *Understanding Death of a Wished-For Child.* OGR Service Corporation, P.O. Box 3586, Springfield, IL 62708, 1979. (booklet)

John D. DeFrain, Leona Martens, and Jan and Warren Stork. *Stillborn— The Invisible Death.* D.C. Heath and Company, Lexington Books, 1986.

Sherokee Ilse. *Empty Arms—Coping After Miscarriage, Stillbirth and Infant Death.* Available from the Compassionate Friends (address above).

John DeFrain, Jaque Tayloer, and Linda Ernst. *Coping with Sudden Infant Death.* Lexington, Mass.: Lexington Books, 1982.

Valentine Dmitriev. *Time to Begin,* 1982. For parents of a child with Down's syndrome. Available by writing: Caring, P.O. Box 400, Milton, WA 98354.

Bernard Ikeler. *Parenting Your Disabled Child.* Philadelphia: Westminster Press, 1986.

Philippa Russell. *The Wheelchair Child: How Handicapped Children Can Enjoy Life to Its Fullest.* Englewood Cliffs, N.J.: Prentice-Hall, 1984.

R. Limbo and S. Wheeler. *When a Baby Dies: A Handbook for Healing and Helping.* La Crosse, Wis.: Resolve Through Sharing, La Crosse Lutheran Hospital/Gundersen Clinic, Ltd., 1986.

S. Borg and J. Lasker. *When Pregnancy Fails: Families Coping with Miscarriage, Stillbirth, and Infant Death.* Boston: Beacon Press, 1981.

H. Norman Wright. *Recovering from the Losses of Life.* Tarrytown, N.Y.: Revell, 1991.

Organizations

Advocates with Persons Who Are Developmentally Disabled (ADD)
P.O. Box 11148
Santa Ana, CA 92711

American Association of Mental Retardation (AAMR)
1719 Kalorama Road, N.W.
Washington, DC 20009
1-800-424-3688

American Association on Mental Retardation—
Religion Division
31 Alexander Street
Princeton, NJ 08542

Association for Retarded Citizens of the United States (ARC)
500 E. Border Street
Suite 300
Arlington, TX 76010

Center for Children with Chronic Illness and Disability
Box 721, UMHC
Harvard Street at East River Road
Minneapolis, MN 55455

Joni and Friends
P.O. Box 3333
Agoura Hills, CA 91301

Support Groups

The Compassionate Friends, Inc.
P.O. Box 3696
Oak Brook, IL 60522
(312) 990-0010

The Candlelighters, Childhood Cancer Foundation
2025 Eye Street, N.W.
Suite 1011
Washington, DC 20006

The National Sudden Infant Death Syndrome Foundation (NSID)
(800) 221-SIDS

National Clearinghouse for SIDS
8201 Greensboro Drive
Suite 600
McLean, VA 22102

Notes

Chapter 1
1. Original source unknown.

Chapter 2
1. Buddy Scott, *Relief for Hurting Parents* (Nashville: Thomas Nelson, 1989), p. 12.
2. R. Scott Sullender, *Losses in Later Life* (New York: Integration Books/Paulist Press, 1989), p. 68.
3. Scott, *Relief for Hurting Parents*, pp. 17-18.
4. Jo Brans, *Mother, I Have Something to Tell You* (New York: Doubleday, 1987), p. 85.
5. James Dobson, *Parenting Isn't for Cowards* (Waco, Tex.: Word, 1987), pp. 184-85, adapted.
6. Gleason L. Archer, *Encyclopedia of Bible Difficulties* (Grand Rapids, Mich.: Zondervan, 1982), p. 253.
7. James Kennedy, *Your Prodigal Child* (Nashville: Thomas Nelson, 1988), pp. 42-43, adapted.
8. Ibid., p. 44.
9. Ibid., p. 45, adapted.
10. Jerry and Mary White, *When Your Kids Aren't Kids Anymore* (Colorado Springs, Colo.: NavPress, 1989), pp. 160-62, adapted.
11. H. Norman Wright, *Always Daddy's Girl* (Ventura, Calif.: Regal, 1989), pp. 281-83, adapted.

Chapter 3

1. "No More Night," Walt Harrah/Word.
2. Dr. Ken Garland, professor, Talbot Graduate School of Theology, La Mirada, California.
3. Used by permission of Mrs. Kathy Madden, Richardson, Texas.

Chapter 4

1. Lilly Singer, Margaret Sirot, and Susan Rodd, *Beyond Loss* (New York: E. P. Dutton, 1988), p. 62.
2. R. Scott Sullender, *Grief and Growth* (New York: Paulist Press, 1985), p. 56.
3. Therese A. Rando, *Grieving* (Lexington, Mass.: Lexington Books, 1988), pp. 11-12, adapted.
4. Ibid., pp. 18-19, adapted.
5. Rosemarie S. Cook, *Parenting a Child with Special Needs* (Grand Rapids, Mich.: Zondervan, 1992), p. 38.
6. Georgia-Witkin, *The Female Stress Syndrome*, 2nd ed. (New York: New Market Press, 1991), p. 91, adapted.
7. Melissa Balmain Weiner, "Stress of Raising Disabled Children Often Leads to Breakup of Families," *Orange County Register,* Nov. 6, 1991, p. A16.
8. Gerald Mann, *When the Bad Times Are Over for Good* (Brentwood, Tenn.: Wolgemuth & Hyatt, 1992), pp. 4-5.
9. Cook, *Parenting a Child with Special Needs,* p. 40.
10. Ann Kaiser Stearns, *Living Through Personal Crisis* (New York: Ballantine, 1984), pp. 85-86.
11. Ann Kaiser Stearns, *Coming Back* (New York: Ballantine, 1988), pp. 16-17.
12. Bob Diets, *Life After Loss* (Tucson, Ariz.: Fisher Books, 1988), p. 27, adapted.
13. Ibid., p. 28, adapted.
14. Charles R. Swindoll, *Growing Strong in the Seasons of Life* (Portland, Oreg.: Multnomah Press, 1983), pp. 274-75.

Chapter 5

1. Carol Staudacher, *Beyond Grief* (Oakland, Calif.: New Harbinger, 1987), pp. 100-101, adapted.
2. Therese A. Rando, *Grieving* (Lexington, Mass.: Lexington Books, 1988), pp. 164-65.
3. Ibid., p. 105, adapted.
4. Ibid., p. 13.
5. Ronald J. Knapp, *Beyond Endurance—When a Child Dies* (New York: Schocken, 1986), p. 45.
6. Ibid., pp. 52-53.
7. Staudacher, *Beyond Grief*, p. 109, adapted.
8. Ibid., p. 113, adapted.
9. Knapp, *Beyond Endurance—When a Child Dies*, p. 103, adapted.
10. Ibid., p. 41.
11. Glen W. Davidson, *Understanding Mourning* (Minneapolis: Augsburg, 1984), p. 59. Used by permission.
12. H. Norman Wright, *Recovering from the Losses of Life* (Tarrytown, N.Y.: Revell, 1991), pp. 48-49, adapted.
13. Knapp, *Beyond Endurance—When a Child Dies* (New York: Schocken, 1986), p. 184, adapted.
14. Ann Kaiser Stearns, *Coming Back* (New York: Ballantine, 1988), p. 172.
15. Knapp, *Beyond Endurance—When a Child Dies*, p. 29.
16. Rando, *Grieving*, p. 169, adapted. Carol Staudacher, *Beyond Grief*, p. 116, adapted.
17. Staudacher, *Beyond Grief*, pp. 117-18, adapted.
18. Rando, *Grieving*, pp. 177-78, adapted.
19. David W. Wiersbe, *Gone But Not Lost* (Grand Rapids, Mich.: Baker, 1992), p. 55.
20. Knapp, *Beyond Endurance—When a Child Dies*, p. 206.
21. Max Lucado, *The Applause of Heaven* (Dallas: Word, 1990), pp. 186-87. Used by permission.
22. Ibid., p. 190.

Chapter 6

1. John DeFrau, "Learning About Grief from Normal Families: SIDS, Stillbirth, and Miscarriage," *Journal of Marital and Family Therapy*, July 1992, p. 223, adapted.
2. Ibid., p. 229, adapted.
3. Therese A. Rando, *Grieving* (Lexington, Mass.: Lexington Books, 1988), pp. 181-83, adapted.
4. As quoted in Delores Kuenning, *Helping People Through Grief* (Minneapolis: Bethany, 1987), p. 130.
5. Carol Staudacher, *Beyond Grief* (Oakland, Calif.: New Harbinger, 1987), p. 104.
6. Rando, *Grieving*, pp. 183-86, adapted.
7. Kuenning, *Helping People Through Grief*, p. 59, adapted.
8. Ibid., p. 60, adapted.
9. Staudacher, *Beyond Grief*, p. 108.
10. Kuenning, *Helping People Through Grief*, p. 63.
11. C. S. Lewis, *A Grief Observed* (New York: Bantam, 1961), p. 9.
12. Staudacher, *Beyond Grief*, p. 227.
13. Dale and Juanita Ryan, *Recovery from Loss* (Downers Grove, Ill.: InterVarsity Press, 1990), pp. 40-41, adapted.
14. Rando, *Grieving*, pp. 281-83, adapted.
15. Ibid., pp. 284-86, adapted.

Chapter 7

1. Rosemarie S. Cook, *Parenting a Child with Special Needs* (Grand Rapids, Mich.: Zondervan, 1992), p. 83.
2. Therese A. Rando, *Grieving* (Lexington, Mass.: Lexington Books, 1988), pp. 170-71, adapted.
3. Ibid., pp. 172-73, adapted.
4. Carol Staudacher, *Beyond Grief* (Oakland, Calif.: New Harbinger, 1987), p. 123, adapted.
5. Charlotte E. Thompson, *Raising a Handicapped Child* (New York: Morrow, 1986), pp. 62-64, adapted.
6. Ibid., p. 66.

7. Rando, *Grieving*, pp. 178-79, adapted.
8. Thomas M. Skric, Jean Ann Summers, Mary Jane Brotherson, and Ann P. Turnbull, "Severely Handicapped Children and Their Brothers and Sisters," *Severely Handicapped Young Children and Their Families*, ed. Jan Blacker (Orlando: Academic Press, 1984), pp. 215-46. As discussed in Cook, *Parenting a Child with Special Needs*, pp. 94-95.
9. Rando, *Grieving*, p. 180, adapted.
10. Gary J. Oliver and H. Norman Wright, *Kids Have Feelings Too* (Wheaton, Ill.: Victor Books, 1993), p. 115.

Chapter 8

1. Therese A. Rando, *Grieving* (Lexington, Mass.: Lexington Books, 1988), pp. 120-24, adapted.
2. Lloyd John Ogilvie, *God's Best for My Life* (Eugene, Oreg.: Harvest House, 1981), p. 9. Used by permission.
3. Robert Veninga, *A Gift of Hope* (Boston: Little, Brown, 1985), p. 150.
4. Marilyn Willett Heavilin, *When Your Dreams Die* (San Bernardino, Calif.: Here's Life, 1990), pp. 39-41.
5. *Los Angeles Times*, Dec. 22, 1991, Metro Section B, pp. 1-2, adapted.
6. Lilly Singer, Margaret Sirot, and Susan Rodd, *Beyond Loss* (New York: E.P. Dutton, 1988), pp. 92-93, adapted.

Chapter 9

1. Therese A. Rando, *Grief, Dying and Death* (Champaign, Ill.: Research Press, 1984), p. 134, adapted.
2. Steve Laroe, "My Infant's Death: A Father's Story," *Glamour*, as quoted in Carol Staudacher, *Men and Grief* (Oakland, Calif.: New Harbinger, 1991), p. 207.
3. Staudacher, *Men and Grief*, pp. 4-12, adapted.
4. Therese A. Rando, ed., *Parental Loss of a Child* (Champaign, Ill.: Research Press, 1986), p. 294, adapted.
5. Michael E. McGill, *The McGill Report on Male Intimacy* (New York: Harper & Row, 1985), p. 176.

6. Staudacher, *Men and Grief*, p. 155.
7. Ibid., pp. 22-25, adapted.
8. Max Lucado, *No Wonder They Call Him the Savior* (Portland, Oreg.: Multnomah Press, 1986), p. 106.
9. William Schatz, *The Compassionate Friends*, as quoted in "Grief of Father," in *Parental Loss of a Child*, ed. Rando, p. 297.
10. H. Norman Wright, *Recovering from the Losses of Life* (Tarrytown, N.Y.: Revell, 1991), pp. 46-48, adapted.
11. Ken Gire, *Incredible Moments with the Savior* (Grand Rapids, Mich.: Zondervan, 1990), pp. 96-97.
12. Roger Witherspoon, "Say, Brother," *Essence*, as quoted in Staudacher, *Men and Grief*, p. 36.
13. Louis Bragman, "Houdini Escapes from Reality," *The Psychoanalytic Review*, as quoted in Staudacher, *Men and Grief*, p. 37.
14. Staudacher, *Men and Grief*, pp. 34-37, adapted.
15. Rando, *Grief, Dying and Death*, p. 136, adapted.
16. Staudacher, *Men and Grief*, p. 155.
17. Marilyn Willett Heavilin, *When Your Dreams Die* (San Bernardino, Calif.: Here's Life, 1990), pp. 27-28.

Chapter 10

1. As quoted in Bob Diets, *Life After Loss* (Tucson, Ariz.: Fisher Books, 1988), p. 148.
2. Charlotte E. Thompson, *Raising a Handicapped Child* (New York: Morrow, 1986), pp. 38-41, adapted.
3. Diets, *Life After Loss*, pp. 150-51, adapted.
4. Betty Jane Wylie, *The Survival Guide for Widows* (New York: Ballantine, 1982), p. 113.
5. Rosemarie S. Cook, *Parenting a Child with Special Needs* (Grand Rapids, Mich.: Zondervan, 1992), p. 45.

Chapter 11

1. Gloria Hope Hawley, *Champions* (Grand Rapids, Mich.: Zondervan, 1974), pp. 122-23.
2. Ibid., p. 124.

3. Delores Kuenning, *Helping People Through Grief* (Minneapolis: Bethany, 1987), p. 203. Quotation within this material is from Daniel Simundson, *Where Is God in My Suffering?* (Minneapolis: Augsburg, 1983), pp. 28-29. Used by permission.

4. Dwight Carlson and Susan Carlson Wood, *When Life Isn't Fair* (Eugene, Oreg.: Harvest House, 1989), p. 52. Used by permission.

5. Don Baker, *Pain's Hidden Purpose* (Portland, Oreg.: Multnomah Press, 1984), p. 72.

6. Lewis Smedes, *How Can It Be All Right When Everything Is All Wrong?* (New York: Harper & Row, 1982), p. 3.

7. Gerald Mann, *When the Bad Times Are Over for Good* (Brentwood, Tenn.: Wolgemuth & Hyatt, 1992), p. 168, adapted.

8. Ibid.

9. Ibid., p. 169.

10. John Killinger, *For God's Sake—Be Human* (Waco, Tex.: Word, 1970), p. 147, as quoted in Richard Exley, *The Rhythm of Life* (Tulsa: Honor Books, 1987), p. 108. Used by permission.

11. H. Norman Wright, *Recovering from the Losses of Life* (Tarrytown, N.Y.: Revell, 1991), pp. 128-38, adapted.

12. R. Scott Sullender, *Losses in Later Life* (New York: Integration Books/Paulist Press, 1989), pp. 142-43.

13. Letter reprinted by permission of Sherrie Eldridge, Indianapolis, Indiana. Quotation from Robert Munsch, *Love You Forever* (Willowdale, Ont., Can.: Firefly Books, 1986), pp. 1, 23.